Chuck Yeager: First man to fly faste
Gaffney, Timothy

Daniels County Library

P9-DVH-655

DATE DUE

AUG 1 2 1992	
AUG 2 0 1992	
DEC 5 1992	
JAN 2 1999	
JUL 0 2 1999	
OCT 2 1 1999	
JUL 2 3 2014	

BRODART, INC.   Cat. No. 23-221

Chuck Yeager

First Man to Fly
Faster than Sound

by Timothy R. Gaffney

 CHILDRENS PRESS®
CHICAGO

PICTURE ACKNOWLEDGMENTS

AP/Wide World Photos—Frontispiece, pages 2, 14, 69 (2 photos), 70, 71,
72 (2 photos), 73, 112
Department of the Air Force—8, 42, 68, 74
Cover illustration by Len W. Meents

Library of Congress Cataloging in Publication Data

Gaffney, Timothy R.
  Chuck Yeager: first man to fly faster than sound.

  Includes index.
  Summary: Surveys the life of the country boy from West
Virginia who became a great pilot, ending his career as an
Air Force brigadier general with more than 10,000 hours of
flying time in some 180 different aircraft.
  1. Yeager, Chuck, 1923-   —Juvenile literature.
2. Air pilots—United States—Biography—Juvenile
literature. [1. Yeager, Chuck, 1923-   . 2. Air pilots.]
I. Title. II. Series.
TL540.Y4G34   1986   623.74′6048′0924 [B] [92]   86-9555
ISBN 0-516-03223-2

Copyright © 1986 by Regensteiner Publishing Enterprises, Inc.
All rights reserved. Published simultaneously in Canada.
Printed in the United States of America.
  3 4 5 6 7 8 9 10 R 95 94 93 92 91 90 89 88 87

To Mom and Dad, who brought me up in Dayton

ACKNOWLEDGMENTS

The following people were instrumental in helping me collect information for this book: Paul Bowles; Pansy Lee Yeager Cummings; Patty Clay, *Huntington Herald-Dispatch*; Don Haley, Edwards Air Force Base; Sam Koontz; Donald Rahn; Bob Rahn; Hettie Rousch, Hamlin-Lincoln County Public Library; Colonel Larry G. Van Pelt, USAF; and Susie Mae Yeager.

Table of Contents

Glamorous Glennis, the X-1 Yeager flew when he broke the sound barrier.

Chapter 1

"FIRING FOUR"

It was waiting for him somewhere up in the thin, blue desert sky. Nobody knew for sure what it was. Nobody could see it. Nobody had ever touched it. Nobody was sure it *could* be touched.

It was something that nobody knew about until people started flying at high speeds, close to the speed at which sound itself moves through the air. As a pilot approached this mysterious threshold, his control stick would begin to shake. Suddenly, his airplane would pitch out of control, and the screaming wind would rip it to pieces. Good pilots had died this way.

As an airplane flew faster and faster through the air, the air had less time to move out of the way. Near the speed of sound, the airplane would compress the air into shock waves that interfered with the controls and put dangerous stresses on the airplane. Some people believed that the air would compress into an invisible but deadly wall of pressure against an airplane flying at the speed of sound. One scientist called it a "brick wall in the sky." Most people called it the sound barrier, and, on this morning of October 14, 1947, high in the cloudless sky over California's Mojave Desert, it was waiting for Chuck Yeager.

Charles Elwood Yeager was just twenty-four years old, but he was already used to danger in the air. As a combat pilot in World War II, which had just ended two years ago, he had shot down thirteen enemy airplanes in the skies over Europe. He had been shot down over France and wounded, but he had evaded capture and returned to fight some more.

Yeager didn't believe there was any wall in the sky. In his opinion, the only limits to speed were in the design of an airplane and in the pilot's abilities. If you were a good enough flier, and if you had a good enough airplane, why, you could fly faster than sound without any trouble—or so he hoped.

He believed he could do it. He had come to this barren place in the desert, Muroc Air Force Base it was called, to find out if the airplane could do it.

The airplane was an orange, bullet-shaped thing called the XS-1, or the X-1. It wasn't big. It was long and low, and it sat on tiny landing gear. Its wings were short and straight.

It had no propellers. It had no gaping air inlets for jet engines. The X-1 was a different kind of airplane. It was a rocket airplane. The four chambers on its rear end burned diluted alcohol and liquid oxygen—oxygen cooled to 290 degrees below zero, Fahrenheit. The engines had a terrific kick, but they ate through their fuel supply in just two and a half minutes.

To save its precious fuel, the X-1 was carried aloft beneath a B-29 bomber, tucked halfway into the B-29's large bomb bay. At the right moment, the B-29 would drop the X-1, and the X-1's pilot would fire the rockets. Before each test, the X-1 had to be eased into a shallow pit on the flight line so the B-29 could roll over it for loading.

Yeager had flown the airplane before. He trusted it. He had to: it didn't have an ejection seat.

Dawn was just streaking the desolate horizon, but the X-1 was already down in its pit. A ground crew was filling its tanks. The chill from the liquid oxygen turned the orange airplane's belly white with frost. Cold vapors swirled eerily around it.

The airplane was in good shape, but Yeager wasn't. Two nights ago he had gone horseback riding, and the horse had thrown him. He had cracked two right ribs, and pain stabbed in his side. He could hardly use his right arm.

At first he didn't see how he could secure the door to the X-1's cockpit: the locking lever was on the right. But he didn't want to cancel the flight. Instead, he quietly went to the flight engineer, a good friend named Jack Ridley. Ridley added a piece of broom handle to the lever, making it easier to close.

Yeager climbed into the B-29. Its four engines thundered, spinning their propellers into a blur. Mother ship and rocket plane lifted into the sky. At seven thousand feet, Yeager went into the bomb bay and down a ladder. The doorway to the X-1's cockpit was below the B-29, exposed to the noise and the blasting wind. The brown desert was visible beneath his feet. Clutching the ladder, he slid feetfirst into the cockpit. Ridley lowered the door and pushed it into place. Yeager grasped the broomstick with his left hand, gritted his teeth, and shoved it. The lever locked.

The B-29 continued to climb in a wide spiral. The desert fell away. The dry, flat beds of ancient lakes mottled its surface. When the desert was dry, as it was now, the lake beds baked in the sun until they were as hard as concrete. They made the world's biggest runways, and Yeager would need the room: after it spent its fuel, the X-1 turned into a high-speed glider. There was no telling where he might have to land. And if the sound barrier was up there—if Yeager hit the brick wall in the sky and fell back to the desert—well, there wasn't much down there to hurt but a few Joshua trees.

The B-29 reached twenty-six thousand feet and leveled out. Yeager sat in the cramped cockpit, checking instruments. His side ached. The liquid-oxygen tank behind the cockpit chilled him.

His headset crackled with Ridley's voice. "You all set?" Yeager gave a curt reply. "Let's get it over with."

The B-29 dipped into a shallow dive to pick up speed. The pilot counted down the seconds. At zero, Yeager heard the bomb shackle clang and felt a jolt. The X-1 dropped from the dark bomb bay and sudden daylight blasted the cockpit. The sun looked like a ball of fire just outside the canopy. Yeager felt his weight leave him as the airplane fell free.

He kept calm and went to work. "Firing four," he radioed. He lit one rocket right after another. The blast of power felt like a kick in the back as the X-1 leaped skyward.

Yeager was on his way. He was going to charge up there and punch a hole right through that old sound barrier. If he succeeded, he would make history as the first man ever to fly faster than sound. If he failed . . .

Failure was a word he didn't use.

Susie Yeager gives her son a kiss. She still lives in the West Virginia town of Hamlin.

Chapter 2

HAMLIN

You have to want to go to Hamlin, West Virginia, to get there. It's a small town of about one thousand people nestled deep in the wooded hills southeast of Huntington. No major highway leads directly to it. The only highway through the town is State Route Three, a two-lane road.

At the edge of town along State Route Three stands a big white sign with blue letters. The sign proclaims:

Hamlin
Hometown of Charles Yeager
First Man to Fly Faster Than Sound

In the center of town, a local bank displays a bronze bust of Yeager and a model of the X-1 rocket plane in its lobby. A portrait and some prints of planes he has flown hang on a wall in Hamlin High School.

Hamlin may call itself Yeager's hometown, but it isn't the place of his birth. He was born February 13, 1923. At that time his parents, Albert Hal and Susie Mae Yeager, lived in a white farmhouse up the Mud River from Hamlin. They were closer to the tiny community of Myra. Yeager's family moved from Myra to Hamlin in 1927, according to his sister

Pansy Lee Yeager Cummings. They lived in a white house that overlooked the town.

Hal Yeager was the owner of Yeager Drilling Company, a small company that drilled natural-gas wells. Susie Mae was busy mothering five children—Roy (the oldest), Charles, Doris Ann, Pansy Lee, and Hal, Jr., the youngest. Neighbors described both Hal and Susie as good, kind people. Susie Yeager was and is a religious woman who frowns on alcoholic drinks. Hal Yeager died in 1963.

Some people in Hamlin still remember Chuck Yeager as a boy whom they called Charles or Charlie. They say his worldwide fame hasn't changed him. One who remembers him well is Homer Hager, Jr. or "Drummer," as everybody in Hamlin has called him, since he played drums in the high school band. "He's just a old country boy," Drummer Hager says. Drummer lived close to him, went through school a year ahead of him, and still sees him when he comes to town.

But how well anyone in Hamlin really knew young Charles is hard to tell. "He wasn't a real mixer. He liked to be out in the woods hunting or fishing," recalled Sam Koontz, a mortician who was in school a few years ahead of Charles. Yeager tended to daydream in school, others recall, and he was better at math and technical subjects than he was at English.

To a boy in the late 1920s and 1930s, the hills and hollows around Hamlin must have seemed like unexplored wilderness. "Charlie and I, we stayed in the woods all the time," Drummer Hager recalled. "Back in these hills, we'd climb a tree and ride the branches right down to the bottom. We'd grab vines and swing out over cliffs."

There were special places in those woods where Charlie and Drummer liked to go. Two of them were rocky outcrops on the tops of steep ridges. The boys called them Whitaker Rock and Maul Rock. Whitaker Rock was tabletop flat, a great place to camp out with a blanket and some food. Maul Rock was a vertical, club-shaped rock—just the place, or so it seemed, for a boy to carve his initials.

The woods also meant food for the table, whether it was hickory nuts and pawpaws, or game that all the Yeager boys hunted. Charles was shooting a .22 rifle by the time he was six, and even then he lived up to the original German meaning of his family name: Jäger, or hunter. He had remarkable eyesight, much better than 20/20 vision, and he could draw a bead on a target that others didn't even see.

Guns meant food and sport, but they also meant tragedy for the Yeager family, as Charles revealed more than fifty years later in his autobiography *Yeager*, coauthored by Leo Janos. When Charles was four, he and six-year-old Roy were playing with their father's shotgun. Roy found some shells, loaded the gun, and accidently fired it. The 12-gauge blast hit two-year-old Doris Ann and killed her.

Had guns just been sporting weapons, a family that suffered the Yeagers' loss might have sold their rifles or locked them away, but guns were tools to the Yeagers. After the accident, their father made sure that Roy and Charles learned how to handle guns safely. Shooting was second nature to Charles by the time he went to war.

Quiet as he seemed to others, Charles had a sense of mischief, a quality that would reveal itself in the most dramatic ways when he flew high-powered airplanes. Once when they were about twelve, Drummer Hager recalled, Charles' father was fermenting homemade blackberry wine in a stone cellar. "Charlie and I got in there and drank some of it," Drummer said. It had not fermented long enough to become alcoholic, so the boys did not get drunk. "But we got a whipping just the same," he said.

Charles showed more interest in mechanical things as he grew older. Because of his father's drilling business, he was constantly around pumps, motors, and other machinery. H. Leon Hager, an automobile dealer and a private pilot, once told a newspaper reporter that Yeager spent many hours in his garage under the hoods of cars. It was another hint of the direction his future would take.

Shooting and mechanics were two skills that Yeager would use throughout his career, but there were other qualities he picked up in Hamlin, especially the bluntly honest, no-nonsense attitude often found in West Virginia. He was raised to say exactly what he thought, a habit that could startle someone used to more subtle ways. If he made up his mind that he didn't like somebody, someplace, or something, that was that. On the other hand, his friends knew that they could count on him for any kind of help.

Yeager broke no academic records in Hamlin High School. He played football and basketball, played trombone in the marching band, and dated a few girls, but marriage wasn't in his plans.

He got his first taste of military life in the summers after his sophomore and junior years—1939 and 1940. He attended the Civilian Military Training Camp at Fort Benjamin Harrison in Indiana. It was an Army program to help prepare civilians for military service.

As Yeager neared graduation, Hamlin began to feel too small to him. Its neighborly people and endless woods made Hamlin a great place to grow up, but it just didn't offer much for a restless young man. He worked in a pool hall after graduating from high school. He also worked for a local photographer, cleaning up the studio.

He heard more and more about the Army. Friends who had joined the service dropped back in town. They told him that he could go to school in the Army to learn skills that could help him find a good job.

The older people in Hamlin talked about the war overseas. J.D. Smith, a local attorney and former state senator, told Yeager how Germany was sweeping across Europe, first taking Poland, then The Netherlands and France. It was locked in battle with Great Britain in the skies over the North Sea and the English Channel. It was only a matter of time, Smith warned him, until the United States would have to join the conflict. Yeager had grown up listening to Smith and admiring his wisdom. He thought about what he said.

When an Army recruiter came to town, Yeager talked to him. The recruiter told him that he could be a pilot. He didn't need to have a college education or to be an officer; the Army Air Corps had started something called the Flying Sergeant program. He could join up, go through basic training, then sign up for flight school. He'd become a flier and a sergeant and make a sergeant's pay.

Yeager made up his mind. He wanted to be a pilot. On September 12, 1941, he went up to Huntington and had himself sworn into the Army.

He had no way of knowing that he would become not only a pilot but one of history's greatest and that his military career would end not after a few years as a sergeant but after thirty-four years at the rank of brigadier general.

Chapter 3

SILVER WINGS

Chuck Yeager got out of Hamlin, all right. For the next two years, the Army moved him from one airfield to another, all of them on the other side of the continent from Hamlin. After that he would be shipped across the ocean to foreign lands. The country boy had left his hills and hollows far behind.

His first assignment was at Ellington Field, Texas. There, the Army put him through two months of marching, saluting, and infantry drilling. This was basic training, where raw recruits like Yeager were turned into soldiers. Then the Army assigned him to learn aircraft mechanics at Moffet Field in San Mateo County, California, south of San Francisco.

He was learning mechanics at Moffet when a fateful day came. On December 7, 1941, Japanese airplanes attacked an American naval base in Hawaii—Pearl Harbor. The blow crippled America's fleet in the Pacific Ocean. The United States declared war on Japan. Japan was an ally of Germany, and Germany declared war on the United States. So did Italy, another German ally. America entered World War II.

After three months at Moffet Field, the Army moved

Yeager again. He went to Victorville Army Base in southern California, across the San Gabriel Mountains from Los Angeles. Private Yeager became Corporal Yeager, his first step up in rank. He also became a crew chief. A crew chief leads a crew of mechanics that keeps an airplane in flying condition.

His crew worked on an AT-11. It had two engines and a stubby nose. The Army Air Force used it to train bomber crews. It was aboard an AT-11, half a year after deciding to join the Army and to learn to fly, that Yeager got his first flight. It was less than glorious.

An AT-11 pilot asked Yeager if he wanted to come along on a short flight. They climbed into the cockpit. The engines roared and the airplane climbed into the sky. Everything shrank below them. Houses looked like toys; roads looked like ribbons. Yeager felt the ship moving in the air, bumping and sagging in the invisible currents, constantly moving one way or another. He got airsick.

That happened the first few times he flew. He still wanted to fly, though. He wasn't going to let a few bad rides turn him away, not after he'd come this far, joining the Army and everything. As a mechanic, he knew airplanes inside and out. He knew more about how they worked than did most pilots.

In July 1942, the Army decided to give him his chance. It moved him again, south to Ryan Field in Hemet, California, for flying school. Ground lessons came first—classroom stuff. The classes drilled home the most basic but most important facts: how airplanes fly. Yeager became familiar with all the basics of aircraft and flight. Then he flew, and he didn't get sick anymore.

His first training plane was a Ryan. It sat two—an instructor and a student behind him—in open cockpits. The roar of the wooden propeller and the blast of the slipstream would pour over them while they flew. The Ryan wasn't very fast—125 miles per hour, tops—but it gave beginners a taste of flying.

Yeager's instructor taught him how to take off, to turn, to find his way from one place to another, and to land again. Then he flew solo. Nobody was with him as he roared into the sky, and nobody was there to grab the controls if he goofed up his landing approach. He had to do it right, or else. He did it right.

After mastering the basics, he went to Luke Field (now Luke Air Force Base) in Arizona, near Phoenix. There, he learned to be a combat pilot, a warrior of the air. He learned how to attack targets in the air and on the ground. He learned how to aim his airplane like a weapon and how to fire its machine guns. He learned the tricky maneuvers needed for dogfighting with enemy airplanes or for dodging antiaircraft fire from the ground.

On March 10, 1943, the Army gave him a pair of silver wings. He was a pilot now, but he wasn't a flying sergeant. The Air Corps had started a new program that made pilots more like officers. Yeager became what the Army called a flight officer.

His next assignment was to a combat unit, the 363rd Fighter Squadron of the 357th Fighter Group. It was a new group stationed in Tonopah, Nevada.

Tonopah sprang up in the barren mountains of Nevada during the silver-mining days of the last century. The silver was gone, but the parched mountains, canyons, and endless stretches of desert were still there. It was a forbidding place, with tar-paper shacks for barracks and the constant desert wind for company. But to Yeager it was heaven. He had a combat plane and good buddies who were combat pilots like himself. All they wanted to do was fly hard and fast, and that was what they were supposed to do.

They flew P-39 Airacobras. The "P" stood for "Pursuit," an early term for what we now call fighter planes. The P-39 was a little unusual. Its propeller was on the end of its snout, but the engine was back behind the cockpit. That made room for a powerful cannon that pointed out the nose of the plane. The cannon made the P-39 deadly against ground targets such as tanks.

In their P-39s they sliced through canyons and roared at hundreds of miles per hour across the desert "on the deck," barely above the ground. They wheeled and soared and blasted away at targets on the gunnery and bombing ranges. All they wanted to do was fly, and they flew all the time.

Yeager was a pilot, but now he was also a combat pilot. Only the best pilots got to be combat pilots. He worked hard to sharpen the skills he would need when the Army sent his squadron into combat.

They were in Tonopah for three months, then moved to Oroville in northern California. His life didn't change, he still flew all the time, but in Oroville he met a young woman named Glennis Faye Dickhouse. Years later, the name Glennis would find a place in the National Air and Space Museum. But at that time she was just a volunteer for the United Service Organization, better known as the USO, which provided activities and entertainment for people in the military services.

If it wasn't love at first sight, it was close to it. They saw each other constantly, or at least as much as Yeager's military life made possible. By the time his squadron was transferred to Casper, Wyoming, they had decided not to call it the end. But, for Yeager, on two occasions it very nearly was the end.

The first was on October 16, 1943. As he was landing, his gear failed. His P-39 slid down the runway on its belly. The plane was a mess, but he wasn't hurt.

The next accident happened on October 21. It was worse. He was leading eleven P-39s at eighteen thousand feet on practice raids against bombers. He spotted a flight of B-24s—big, four-engine bombers—flying far below them. Yeager led the pursuit planes into a dive. Staging a mock attack, the P-39s hurtled past the bombers.

Then something in Yeager's airplane blew apart. He saw fire under his seat. He bailed out of the burning plane and pulled the rip cord on his parachute. The chute popped open and jerked him with a yank that knocked him out. He woke up in the base hospital with a cracked vertebra. It was a painful injury, but he recovered.

Back in Oroville, Glennis could do little but worry and write. Soon she had a new reason for worry and a new address for her letters, an airfield in England. Yeager had been sent to war.

Chapter 4

MISSING IN ACTION

In the beginning of 1944, Yeager and the 357th Fighter Group were stationed at Raydon Wood Airdrome in the county of Suffolk, on the eastern side of England.

Germany held the European coast from the North Sea down to Spain. Beyond the occupied lands of Holland, Belgium, and France lay Germany itself, the heart of the Nazi threat. Already, Allied bombers were striking at German forces in the occupied countries and at the industrial centers in Germany. The Luftwaffe, Germany's air force, had been damaged, but it was still dangerous. The Allied bombers went without the protection of combat planes when they flew over Germany because few of the planes on hand could go that far.

War was close, but Yeager and his combat buddies found themselves with no missions and no airplanes. They had left behind their P-39 Airacobras. They learned that they were waiting for a new pursuit plane built by North American Aviation, the P-51 Mustang.

The Mustang was a powerful, racy-looking aircraft. Its four-bladed propeller, a large air scoop under its belly, and the bubble-type canopy of later models made the P-51 stand out. It was fast. Its top speed exceeded four hundred miles per hour. With disposable fuel pods mounted under its wings, the P-51 had enough range to escort bombers on raids over Germany. Finally, its maneuverability and its six .50-caliber machine guns made it a ferocious fighter. The Mustang became one of the most famous fighters of World War II.

But only a few P-51s had arrived, and Yeager, like most of the 357th, had not yet joined the fighting. The group moved to a new location at the end of January. This was Leiston Airfield, near the towns of Leiston and Oxford.

Leiston Airfield had three concrete runways that crossed in the shape of an *A*. Around the airfield ran a concrete taxi strip. Along the taxi strip were concrete pads called hardstands. This was where the airplanes would be parked.

Some of the hardstands had earthen mounds built around them for protection, but most of the airplanes sat in the open. By that time in the war, Germany was too busy defending its homeland from bombers to send many airplanes over England. The 357th suffered only one attack, when a lone German fighter strafed one of the buildings with its machine guns one night. Nobody was hurt.

The pilots lived in metal huts with arched, corrugated roofs. These were called Nissen huts, named after a British engineer who designed them. Iron stoves that burned coal or wood gave them meager heat against the cold, foggy, rainy, or snowy countryside, and somewhere across the frigid North Sea was the war.

At Leiston they received their Mustangs, their wings. Following custom, the pilots named their planes. They painted the names on the sides of their machines, names such as *Old Crow, Spooky, Missouri Armada,* and *Hurry Home Honey.* Yeager knew what he wanted to name his: *Glamorous Glen,* for his sweetheart Glennis.

With their new airplanes came their mission: to protect the waves of B-17 and B-24 bombers of the Eighth Air Force, which were pounding Germany and being pounded by the Luftwaffe. They would take off from their airfield and join the bombers as they reached the coast of France. Then they would fly in their own formations, watching for signs of enemy airplanes.

Yeager flew his first mission during that gray winter. In a predawn briefing, he and the other pilots learned that they were to escort bombers in a raid on Hamburg, Germany. Yeager, always impatient for action, no doubt wanted to find out what combat was like, but no doubt he also felt a tight knot of fear in his stomach.

When the briefing was over, they went to their airplanes. The Mustangs were already being prepared by their ground crews. As the morning turned from black to gray, the Mustangs at Leiston Airfield growled to life. Their propellers spun into angry blurs. One after another they roared into the sky, gathered into V-shaped formations and flew off to meet the bombers.

They saw clouds of flak—exploding shells from antiaircraft guns—but no fighters. All the way to Hamburg and back, Yeager looked for enemy fighters, but he saw nothing.

Yeager flew several more missions, all of them uneventful. Each time, he would set out with excitement and anxiety, wondering if this time he'd see action, pushing aside the thought that he might not come back, and each time he would land back at Leiston without having fired a shot. But that was typical of a combat pilot's life—he never knew if a mission would be dangerous or dull.

He had his first dogfight on March 4, 1944. Bombers were making a daylight raid over Berlin, Germany. As usual, Yeager was flying escort. Then he spotted a German fighter, a Messerschmitt (Me) 109. He dropped his wing tanks, opened the throttle, and dived at it. He went so fast that he overshot the target, but he turned and found the Me-109 diving to escape. Yeager fired his guns, damaged the engine, and saw the pilot bail out of his crippled airplane.

The action wasn't over. Soon he spotted a twin-engine Heinkel (He) 111. He went at it from behind. The Heinkel had a gunner in the rear of the plane. The gunner was shooting at him. Yeager blasted back until the gunner stopped, probably dead. One engine was smoking as the Heinkel entered a cloud and disappeared.

Faced with combat, Yeager had acted according to his nature: confident, determined, unhesitating. His skillful flying and his eagle eyes made him a deadly shot. He had found that killing, and the danger of being killed, didn't even slow him down. "Dogfights are pretty impersonal," he said years later in a *Washington Post* interview. "You never think about the guy in the cockpit. It's all eyesight and tactical advantage. If you're right, it works out. If you aren't, it don't."

The next day, March 5, it didn't work out. Eighth Air Force bombers were hitting Bordeaux in southeastern France this time. Forty-six Mustangs escorted the bombers. Yeager was the last plane in his formation. The bombers made their run on their target, dropped their bombs, and turned for home.

A small group of Focke-Wulf (FW) 190s caught them by surprise. Since Yeager had the last plane in his formation, he was their first target. They had the advantage, and they hammered him.

Twenty-millimeter shells ripped through his Mustang. The canopy blew away, bits of metal flew into his feet, and smoke and fire erupted around him. The airplane dipped a wing and fell into a spin. *Glamorous Glen* was going down in flames.

In Hamlin, the Yeagers heard nothing until a telegram arrived from the War Department. Charles was missing in action. Years later, his sister Pansy Lee recalled how that bit of news seemed to tell them so much and so little at the same time. "We knew that he was missing, but that was all for some time," she said.

Was he dead or alive? There was no way to know. It left them with a dreadful, helpless feeling, especially for Hal, Sr., and Susie Mae. They had lost one child years earlier. Now they feared that they had lost another, and a third, Roy, was in the Navy, facing combat in the Pacific. "It was a rough time for them," Pansy Lee recalled. As the weeks dragged by, they heard nothing more.

Yeager drifted to earth under the canopy of his parachute. He landed in the cover of a forest, gathered up his parachute, and hid. He didn't stay hidden for long, but fortunately it was a French farmer, not a German soldier, who found him. The farmer and his family hid him in their home, knowing they were risking their own lives; if the Germans found him there, they would shoot them all.

His chances of seeing his family or Glennis again weren't good. He had come down about fifty miles from Bordeaux, deep in German-occupied land. He spoke neither French nor German. Somehow, he had to get to Spain, a neutral country, where he would have a chance to get back to England. But the border was more than two hundred miles away, and he had nothing but his wounded feet and a small survival kit.

The French family helped. They hid him for two days, then dressed him in woodsman's clothes, set him on a bicycle, and led him away. They put him in the hands of the Maquis, an organization of French citizens who were secretly resisting their German occupiers and helping the Allies.

For twenty-two days, Yeager hid by day and moved by night, always guided by members of the Maquis. He lived in constant danger of being captured or shot. Eventually, he joined several other American fliers, and the Maquis shepherded them toward Spain.

On March 23, they found themselves close to the border.

Between them and Spain were the snow-covered Pyrenees Mountains and the German patrols.

Their friends gave them knapsacks with some food. There was no more they could do. Yeager and the others set out for the border through deep, wet snow. Eventually, Yeager and another man outdistanced the rest.

Yeager and his companion trudged ahead for four days, wet and cold, fighting exhaustion. On the fourth day they discovered an empty woodsman's cabin. They stumbled gratefully through the door.

While they slept inside, a German patrol passing outside spotted signs of their presence. They opened fire on the cabin. The two fliers dived out a window and tumbled down a long slope to safety, but a bullet had caused a serious wound in the leg of Yeager's companion. He looked dead, but he was breathing. Yeager treated the wound as well as he could.

Spain was on the other side of a ridge. Yeager waited until dark, then began dragging the unconscious man up the slope.

The climb up to the ridge was exhausting. Yeager would plant his feet, take a step, then haul on the limp flier. It was an endless ordeal with no rest. He was afraid that, if he relaxed, he might lose his grip and send his companion sliding back down the slope. He knew that he wouldn't have the strength to go back down for him.

Dawn was breaking when Yeager stumbled onto the ridge. He was exhausted, and the flier was still unconscious, but the route ahead of them was downhill: they were in Spain.

After the ordeal, Yeager would receive a Bronze Star for saving his companion's life. He had acted "with complete disregard for his personal safety," as the citation that came with the Bronze Star put it. He received a Purple Heart for his wounds.

But their troubles weren't quite over. While the wounded man was taken away for treatment and then later sent back to the United States, Yeager reported to a local police station. The police put him in jail.

Jail didn't appeal to Yeager, and the police showed little interest in him. They never bothered to search him, or they would have found a small steel saw blade in his survival kit. The bars on the window were made of soft brass. It took Yeager no time at all to cut through them with his little saw.

The police never tried to track down their fugitive, but apparently they reported his presence to American representatives in Spain. The Americans found him a few days later, staying in the village where he had been arrested. Yeager remained in Spain for another six weeks before he and a number of other fliers were released to the Americans, but he spent no more time in jail. In fact, he returned to cold, gray England with a suntan.

Back in England, Yeager was questioned at length by intelligence officers. They wanted to know everything he had seen or heard. He didn't know it then, in the first few days of June, but the Allied forces were about to launch one of the largest military operations of all time: Operation Overlord. On June 6, 1944, the Allies would return to France for the first time since the start of the war. Crossing the English Channel, battleships would bombard the beaches of Normandy while wave upon wave of troops stormed ashore.

Yeager didn't know about that. All he learned was that his ordeal had earned him a trip back to the United States. In fact, fliers who returned from being shot down were forbidden to fight again in the same area. Military leaders at the highest levels made that rule. They feared that if the fliers were shot down and captured, they would be forced to tell who had helped them and how. That would mean death for people like the French family that had helped Yeager, and it would mean less help for other fliers.

But Yeager protested. He wanted to be with his friends in the 363rd Squadron. He wanted to fly and to fight. There were others like him who felt the same way. They appealed all the way to the Supreme Commander of the Allied Expeditionary Forces, General Dwight D. Eisenhower.

They got their wish eventually, partly because the war was changing. Once friendly forces began rolling across France, there was less risk to the Maquis. And the Air Force still needed good pilots. Yeager was sent back to Leiston and was told he could fly. However, he could only fly around the airfield for practice until his official combat orders reached him.

Somehow, things managed to go awry. Soon after he had returned to Leiston, word came that a B-17 had ditched in the North Sea off the coast of Holland. With most of the squadron away on a mission, only Yeager and three new pilots were available to search for the crewmen and to protect them until help arrived. The airfield's operations officer ordered him to lead the flight.

They spotted some crewmen on a life raft, but Yeager's sharp eyes spotted a lone German bomber flying toward them. He had no orders allowing him to fly combat missions. He really had no business being out there. But there he was, and there was this bomber, a threat to the men in the water and an easy target besides. Yeager shoved on the throttle, closed in behind the bomber, and blasted it with his machine guns until it blew up.

His proficiency caused a minor crisis back at squadron headquarters. Yeager had broken the rules. The squadron commander decided that the best solution was to cover up the whole affair. He gave another pilot credit for shooting down the bomber. It kept Yeager and the officers above him out of trouble, but his official record would always list one less victory than his true score.

It was an irritation, no doubt, but what mattered to Yeager was getting back in the action. On June 19, his combat orders finally came through.

Chapter 5

ACE IN A DAY

The job of a fighter pilot was unique in the war. Unlike foot soldiers or even the members of a bomber crew, the fighter pilot was on his own. He flew alone in his own airplane. On missions over Europe and Germany, he was closed up in his cockpit for hours without relief. He was constantly watching for the tiny specks that might represent enemy fighters, and they might appear anywhere, ahead, behind, above, or below. He had to fly over the treacherous North Sea on the way out and on the way back, and he never knew, heading out, in what condition his plane would be on the return trip over that freezing water.

The fighter pilot depended on his fellow pilots for safety. They flew in formations to protect each other. The smallest formation was the two-airplane element. One pilot would be the element leader and the other would be his wingman. In a dogfight, the element leader would attack. The wingman's job was to protect his leader. Two elements made up a flight, and one of the element leaders was the flight leader. Several flights would make up a squadron, and three squadrons would make up a group. But throughout the group, each pilot was either an element leader or a wingman, protecting or protected by another pilot.

That sense of loneliness, and their need to watch out for one another in the air, tended to make fighter pilots a close-knit group on the ground. If one of them was killed, they mourned the loss together not so much by talking about it as simply by sharing the feeling, perhaps over drinks at a bar in Leiston. They lived together, ate together, and spent their free time together. It wasn't a rule written down some-where, but if you weren't a fighter pilot, you just weren't welcome among them.

Among the fighter pilots were smaller, even more exclu-sive groups. The most exclusive were the pilots with the most combat experience, those who had shot down the most planes or those who had distinguished themselves in some way. As the pilots flew more missions, they encountered more flak, more enemy planes, and more bad weather. They were more likely to experience mechanical failure over the North Sea. As more of their buddies died, their groups grew tighter and more private.

Yeager was in one of these groups. He was one of the original squadron members, and his abilities as a combat pilot were proven. He had even been shot down himself and had come back for more. Not only was he brave, he was a survivor. And he was, as everybody recognized, an excep-tional pilot. "There were a number of real, real good pilots ... but Yeager was a cut above all of 'em, really," recalled Paul L. Bowles, who is now an attorney in Charleston, West Vir-ginia, and who flew in Yeager's squadron. "Yeager was extremely good. . . . Flying seemed to be natural for him . . .

[but] he wasn't cocky. He didn't go around talking about how good he was. If he told you about something, he told you because he wanted you to know."

Yeager and Bowles shared a Nissen hut, but their friendship resulted largely from the fact that they were two West Virginia boys stationed far from home. Yeager drew him into his private circle of friends. "He sort of took me under his wing," Bowles said. "I probably would not have been admitted to that select group if I had not been from West Virginia. Because of that I was taken in, not 100 percent, but I was allowed to eat dinner with them."

When he flew as Yeager's wingman, Bowles noticed that Yeager led his flight better than anyone else he knew. As wingman, Bowles's job was to ignore his own controls and to follow whatever Yeager did, keeping his own Mustang just off Yeager's wingtip. Bowles noticed that Yeager could lead him through maneuvers that he couldn't do on his own. "He would do things that, if I tried to do it myself, I'd stall out," he said.

Not every mission led to a dogfight, as Yeager already knew from his earliest missions. He flew through the summer, but he didn't shoot down another plane until September 13.

On their way home over Germany that day, Yeager spotted an Me-109 in a dive. He plummeted after it at full throttle and closed in fast. So did another Mustang flown by Lieutenant Frank L. Gailer. Yeager fired and saw his bullets hitting the enemy's engine and fuselage. The engine began to smoke as Yeager zoomed past. Gailer continued the attack until the Me-109 hit the ground and exploded.

Yeager's official record credited him with one and a half enemy planes destroyed. He shared half a credit for the Me-109 that he and Gailer had shot down. (Of course, his record didn't show any credit for the German bomber he had shot down in June.) A fighter pilot has to shoot down five enemy airplanes to become an "ace," and, on October 12, Yeager became an ace on one mission.

He was leading his fighter group that day, fifty-four Mustangs in three squadrons. They were escorting bombers on another run over Germany. Taking a squadron ahead to scout for German fighters, Yeager spotted twenty-two Me-109s. He took a squadron and went after them, climbing to keep the sun behind them. It would be hard for an enemy pilot to look into the sun and see the Mustangs coming. None of the fighters seemed to notice as Yeager brought his squadron smoothly into position on their tails.

Yeager closed in on the German fighter that was trailing the pack. Before he could fire, the German pilot rolled his airplane over and bailed out. Yeager shifted his sights to the next airplane, but he, too, parachuted away.

Two planes down and not a shot fired by anybody. Yeager was still ahead of the rest of his squadron. He picked another target. He opened fire and raked its surface, especially the pilot's cockpit. Smoking, the airplane slid out of formation, sank slowly into a dive, and spun out of the sky.

He banked and found another target, closed to within one

hundred yards and skidded to one side, then fired at it from a slight angle. The airplane came apart and then exploded.

Meanwhile, another Me-109 was after Yeager, trying to slide behind his tail. Yeager cut to the right and then back to the left, getting on the Me-109's tail instead. The German pilot tried to pull away, but Yeager followed and shot up his wings and tail. The pilot bailed out.

Yeager received the Silver Star for gallantry and became his squadron's first "ace in a day." His combat record was noticed by his superiors, too. On October 24, Lieutenant Yeager became Captain Yeager.

Chuck, flanked by two buddies, stands in front of his fighter plane at his base in England during World War II.

Chapter 6

THE WARRIOR

Down through history, war has held a strange romantic appeal for many people. Aside from thoughts about patriotism and duty, people are stirred at the sight of brave young men, smartly dressed in their uniforms, marching off to war.

Perhaps one of the oldest and most romantic images is that of the knight in armor, taking on another knight in deadly combat. It is war reduced to its simplest and most romantic form, one man pitting his skills against another, fighting to the death for king and country.

By the twentieth century, that romantic image had little to do with reality. Poison gas, bombs, and long-range artillery replaced the image of dueling knights with widespread death and destruction. There was lttle romance for either soldiers or civilians in an artillery barrage or a bombing raid. The bombs fell on brave soldiers and cowards alike.

Only one kind of soldier in World War II still captured that romantic, one-man-against-another image: the fighter pilot. In the air, combat was still a contest between two warriors. The dogfight was a test of fighting skills, a duel with airplanes.

Before he first climbed into a cockpit, Yeager had been

just an ordinary country boy. But in a fighter plane he became a Lancelot with shining armor. He found that he had special talents that were revealed only in aerial combat; war seemed to be his special calling. "Being a fighter pilot, you're put on earth for one thing—to fight," he told the *Huntington Herald-Dispatch* in 1983.

In a dogfight with another pilot, a fighter pilot either proved himself the better pilot or died. For an adventurous, competitive flier liked Yeager, that was the best kind of flying in the world. It was a bet on who was better, and the bet was one's life. "Combat . . . is probably the ultimate situation for a flier," he said in the November 1983 edition of *Modern Maturity* magazine.

Yeager's future was in fighter planes. In the sky over Germany, he encountered the fighter of the future. It was called the Me-262, and it had jet engines.

The jet engine was a new form of propulsion for airplanes. Until jets, the only way to make an airplane move through the air was by using a piston engine to turn a propeller. The piston engine burned fuel to drive pistons, which turned the shaft that spun the propeller. A jet burned fuel to create a powerful exhaust. The exhaust jetting out the back gave the engine its name.

The jet engine promised smoother flight, more miles for the gallon, and faster speed. Both Germany and England experimented with jet aircraft before World War II. The United States began jet-engine research during the war, with help from the British. But Germany put more effort into its research and put the Messerschmitt 262 into production in 1943. It had a shark-shaped body and slightly swept wings. A jet engine hung under each wing. It was fast, its top speed being rated at 540 miles per hour.

By the time Yeager's squadron began encountering the Me-262, the pilots already knew something about jets. "They weren't mysterious. I remember when I was in flight training school, we read about jet aircraft, but we thought they were 20 years in the future," said Paul Bowles.

So the Me-262 wasn't like a flying saucer suddenly appearing in the sky over Germany. Fighter pilots found that they really had little to fear from it, however; it was so fast that it couldn't maneuver well in dogfights. But, said Bowles, "They were pretty devastating if they got in the stream of bombers. . . . Their technique was to get to the rear of the bomber stream, try to come in out of the sun and just fly up the stream, shooting as they went. There was no way we could catch them if we were behind them." Fast as the Mustang was, a P-51 pilot who chased an Me-262 could only watch as the jet pulled away with a one-hundred-mile-per-hour speed advantage. Nobody in Yeager's group had shot one down.

Yeager's squadron was assigned to guard B-24s on a raid over north central Germany on November 6, 1944. The bombers reached their target and emptied their bomb bays without opposition. When they turned toward home, the fighters left them to hunt for jets.

Before long they spotted five jets below them. Yeager's

was one of two flights that plunged after them. He saw his bullets hit one before the jets pulled away and disappeared in the hazy sky. A few minutes later he spotted them again and fired his guns at the leader. He saw bullets hit, but the planes got away again.

Yeager was far from his own squadron by now. He flew on alone, still looking for the elusive Me-262s. Soon he spotted a large German airfield, the jet air base. Antiaircraft guns fired flak at him as he flew past.

Then he spotted a jet in the air. It was heading for the base, wheels down and, for once, flying slowly as it made its landing approach at about five hundred feet. Yeager was behind it. He dropped his plane to the deck and shoved the throttle. His Mustang screamed toward the jet just above ground level. The flak began bursting around him. He gave the jet one short burst, then pulled hard on the stick. The Mustang roared straight up, away from the deadly flak. Yeager looked down and saw the jet crash in a field short of the runway. A wing flew off and the plane caught fire.

Yeager was the first in his group to destroy a jet fighter. It earned him the Distinguished Flying Cross. (A few months after Yeager, Bowles also shot down an Me-262.)

More jets were appearing, but most of Germany's dwindling air force still was made up of piston-engine fighters. Near the end of that month, Yeager's group ran into one of the biggest swarms of enemy fighters it had ever seen.

The P-51s were out to tackle enemy fighters and to strafe ground targets north of Berlin on November 27, when they spotted clouds of Me-109s and FW-190s. Leading the flight, Yeager climbed and brought the Mustangs into attack position behind a swarm of more than 150 FW-190s. He attacked the nearest plane. The German plane dived and then tried to climb and turn, but Yeager kept him in his sights. He fired, and the FW-190's tail blew off.

Yeager turned back for more. The German formation was above him, but one FW-190 jumped on his tail. Yeager whipped his Mustang back and fired at him from one hundred yards. The German plane pitched into a dive and then exploded.

Again he climbed back to the Germans. Closing from behind, he got on the tail of a third FW-190. It tried to turn, but Yeager's turn was sharper and he raked it with his machine guns. The pilot bailed out.

Again he went after the formation, and he saw a German plane trying to circle behind him. Yeager turned at him and fired a burst into the canopy. The cockpit filled with flames and the plane lurched into a dive. Yeager turned back for another round, but by then the German formation had been scattered by the P-51s.

It was a wild battle, but it was decidedly one-sided: Yeager was one of several pilots who shot down two, three, or four planes. The battle cost the Germans twenty-eight FW-190s and three Me-109s. The Americans suffered only one loss, Lieutenant Frank Gailer, and he was accidently shot down by another Mustang. (Gailer bailed out and was taken prisoner but continued his Air Force career after the war.)

Yeager's last mission, his sixty-fourth, was on January 14, 1945. It was also the last mission of his friend Bud Anderson. On this mission, the 357th was to escort bombers on a bombing run to Derben, a suburb of Berlin. Yeager and Anderson were assigned to fly their last missions as alternates—they would fill in if anyone else had to turn back with engine trouble. Nobody did, so, when the group reached Europe, Yeager and Anderson broke away for their own adventure.

They flew to Switzerland and cruised over the majestic, snow-covered Alps like tourists. Their airplanes carried extra fuel in throwaway tanks under the wing; they dropped the tanks on Mount Blanc and strafed the mountain until their wings were streaked with gunpowder. Then they flew home by way of Paris.

The rest of the group was already home when Yeager and Anderson landed and taxied to their hardstands. Everyone on the ground was excited. After Yeager and Anderson had peeled away, the 357th had encountered an enormous swarm of 130 or more German fighters. The group had lost only four planes and claimed 57½, earning it a Distinguished Unit Citation. Yeager and Anderson had clobbered a mountain.

Chapter 7

JET JOCKEY

After leaving England, Chuck Yeager and Bud Anderson flew straight to California to pick up their girlfriends. When Yeager met Glennis for the first time in more than a year, he bluntly told her that he was taking her back to Hamlin to meet his family. Without saying so, he was proposing marriage. Glennis understood, and for the next three days they rode a train across America to West Virginia.

Hamlin gave Yeager a homecoming parade and held a celebration in the high school gym. He was the pride of Lincoln County.

The Yeagers appraised Glennis and approved the marriage. They held the wedding in the Yeagers' home on February 26, 1945. Since Glennis' parents were in California, Yeager arranged for his old mentor, J.D. Smith, to give her away.

The war was over for Yeager and Anderson, but it wasn't easy for them to adjust to a slower, less dangerous pace. The Army assigned them as flight instructors at Perrin Field in Texas. After combat, this was boring stuff. They hated it. Instead of helping fledgling cadets learn to become fighter pilots, Yeager would spar with Anderson, spinning and looping until their students were airsick. At home, Glennis was pregnant with their first child, and she felt ill most of the time.

A new regulation delivered Yeager from Perrin Field. It allowed former prisoners of war or those who had escaped capture to choose an assignment at whatever base they wanted. The Yeagers decided that the best choice would be anyplace close to Hamlin, where Susie Yeager could give Glennis some support during her pregnancy. The closest base turned out to be Wright Field near Dayton, Ohio, a good day's drive from Hamlin but the closest they could get. Yeager transferred to Wright Field in July 1945.

Wright Field (now a part of Wright-Patterson Air Force Base) was the home of the Air Corps' test-pilot school and headquarters of its aircraft development and testing program. Dayton had been an important center of aviation research from the time that two Dayton brothers, Orville and Wilbur Wright, invented the airplane. Wright Field was named in their memory.

As important as his move to Wright Field would be, Yeager would look back on the time with a certain amount of bitterness. He and Glennis could find no home or apartment to rent anywhere around the field. Wartime demand for workers had swelled the local population and caused a severe housing shortage.

Glennis moved in with her husband's parents in Hamlin while Yeager lived in bachelors' quarters at the field. Reunited for just six months since Yeager's return from war, Chuck and Glennis were split apart again. Yeager flew down on weekends when he could, landing in Huntington, the nearest airport. Those weekend visits came too far apart and were far too brief. But it was just the beginning of a lifetime of inconvenient housing and forced separations that they would endure throughout his career.

Still, Wright Field was a flier's dream. Almost any kind of airplane could be found at the flight-test division. As an assistant maintenance officer, Yeager's job was to test each airplane after it underwent repairs or maintenance work. There were always airplanes waiting to be tested, and Yeager flew all the time.

Yeager made his first jet flight within weeks of his arrival. He took the controls of a P-80 Shooting Star, the first U.S. jet fighter to be produced for regular duty. It was a silver jet with straight wings and a single engine. Its speed astonished Yeager: it could cruise along at 550 miles per hour, faster than his P-51 could go in a full-power dive. It was also trickier to handle because flying at jet speeds meant everything happened faster. But he flew constantly and soon became a crack jet pilot.

He didn't miss an opportunity to show Hamlin what he was doing. Hamlin, so remote from Dayton by automobile, was just minutes away by jet. Yeager would dash down to West Virginia in a P-80 and roar low over the houses. Those shingle-raising fly-overs are still the talk of the town. "He would scare me to death," his mother recalled in 1985. "My knees would turn to water." (More than four decades after he left home to be a pilot, Susie Mae Yeager was still the worrying mother: "I wish he didn't fly so much," she said.)

But Hamlin was not the only place where his flying skills were noticed. Watching him was Colonel Albert Boyd, chief of Wright Field's flight-test division. Boyd was an officer in the traditional mold: he believed in buttoned pockets, polished buckles, and gleaming shoes. But he was also an accomplished test pilot, and he saw test-pilot material in Yeager. Boyd had plans for him, and he would have bigger plans in the future. At Wright Field and elsewhere, a bold project was taking shape to challenge the sound barrier.

Efforts to make airplanes fly faster and faster had continued throughout the war. The end of war brought no end to that effort.

Germany had surrendered in May 1945. In August, U.S. B-29 bombers dropped two atomic bombs on Japan, forcing its surrender. But World War II had changed the balance of powers among nations, and U.S. leaders saw new threats.

The United States and the Soviet Union had been allies during World War II, but after its end the two countries treated each other almost as enemies. The Soviet Union was trying to expand its influence over other countries, and the United States was trying to contain it. The United States emerged from the war as the world's most powerful nation, but the Soviet Union began working hard to build up its own military strength, which included atomic weapons.

World War II had proved the importance of air power, and nuclear weapons made it the most potent of all military forces. It was obvious that the country with the fastest bombers and fighters would hold a tremendous and frightening advantage over all others.

But there was a problem. The problem was the sound barrier. The danger in flying near the speed of sound had become evident early in World War II, when researchers on both sides developed ever faster airplanes. On both sides, pilots had learned about it the hard way.

In the United States, Lockheed test pilot Ralph Virden died in 1941 when he tried to test dive a new fighter plane at more than five hundred miles per hour from fifteen thousand feet. He was examining the strange buffeting and pitching tendency that another pilot had observed on the airplane, a P-38 Lightning. But the buffeting suddenly ripped the tail off the airplane, which spun wildly to the ground and took Virden with it.

That same year in Germany, Messerschmitt test pilot Heini Dittmar narrowly escaped the same fate. He was flying an experimental rocket plane, the Me-163. When his airspeed gauge read 623 miles per hour, he suddenly noticed a violent buffeting of his control surfaces. The airplane pitched into a dive. He cut off the rocket, the airplane slowed, and suddenly his controls worked normally again.

In Britain, the Royal Aircraft Establishment probed the speed of sound by pushing Spitfire fighters into very steep, high-speed dives. The Spitfire managed to reach nine-tenths the speed of sound, the closest any propeller-driven airplane came in World War II. But even the Spitfire could not reach the sound barrier.

What was happening? The airplanes were entering what scientists call the transonic region. An airplane wing's curved surface produces lift by forcing air to move faster over the top of the wing than underneath it. In the transonic range, the airplane itself is flying at subsonic speed, but the air moving over the top of the wing becomes supersonic. The mixture of supersonic and subsonic airstreams creates a violent but invisible wake behind the wing. At the same time, the speeding airplane pushes on the air ahead of it, compressing the air against its surfaces. Shock waves crawl across the wings. The airplane's controls no longer work normally, and the turbulent airflow exerts tremendous forces on the airframe itself.

Airplanes approaching the speed of sound tended to pitch down all at once. Pilots who tried to pull up the nose put too much stress on the tail, already feeling the powerful wake from the wings. The tremendous forces wrenched the tails right off some airplanes.

Studying the speed of sound was frustrating work in the 1940s. Wind tunnels of scale models didn't work well at transonic speeds; the shock waves interfered with the tests. Test-flying real airplanes into the transonic region was dangerous. Models dropped from high altitudes yielded only a little information.

For a while, transonic flight seemed to be a problem only during high-speed dives. Propeller-driven aircraft lacked the power to reach the speed of sound in normal flight; the propeller itself lost efficiency rapidly as it neared transonic speed. But jet engines didn't have that problem, and jet airplanes came perilously close to the speed of sound. If only a solution could be found to the violent forces in the transonic region, fantastic speeds might be possible.

Some scientists questioned whether anything could fly at the speed of sound. They believed that the pressures might continue to build up until they became infinite. A British aircraft designer, W.F. Hilton, described the speed of sound as a barrier. Reporters picked up the idea and created the phrase "sound barrier." Other researchers called it a sonic wall or, even more harshly, a "brick wall in the sky."

But not every scientist was convinced that the sound barrier existed. One was Ezra Kotcher, a scientist working at Wright Field. Kotcher and others had conducted wind-tunnel tests that showed the familiar shock waves in the transonic region, but at supersonic speed, beyond the so-called sound barrier, the problem seemed to go away.

In 1942, Kotcher published a paper recommending that the Army develop a rocket plane to test the sound barrier. Jet engines were still not powerful enough to propel an airplane faster than sound; Kotcher thought that the quickest solution would be to use rockets. The Army wanted a solution to the sound barrier problem as quickly as possible. Following Kotcher's advice, it awarded a contract for a rocket engine.

Getting a contract for an airplane to go with it was another matter: Airplane manufacturers were reluctant to tackle the design challenges of a supersonic airplane.

On November 30, 1944, Kotcher received a surprising offer from a visitor to his Wright Field office. The visitor was Robert J. Woods, design chief for Bell Aircraft. Woods told him that Bell wanted to build an airplane to study flight at the speed of sound. Then and there, they made the first plans for a supersonic project.

Woods called his home office to give the news to the head of Bell Aircraft, Lawrence D. Bell. "You'd better sit down and relax," Woods told him. "I've got some news. I've just committed you to the production of an 800-mile-an-hour plane."

It was a bold move, but Larry Bell liked to be known for boldness. His company had developed America's first experimental jet, the XP-59A. It knew that jets and rockets could take airplanes to the sound barrier. What had to be known, if the airplane industry was to keep making faster machines, was what would happen when they met the sonic wall.

Yeager had heard about the sound barrier. In high-speed dives in his Mustang, he had felt the plane begin to shake and felt his controls lock as the airplane flirted with the transonic region. Only by pulling back forcefully on his control stick could he bring the airplane out of such a dive. In the new jets, too, he learned to avoid getting too close to the sound barrier.

He didn't know that his career was about to take a new turn and that it would have everything to do with the sound barrier.

Chapter 8

"BRICK WALL IN THE SKY"

On a summer day in 1947, two silver jets banked gracefully into their final landing approach over Wright Field. Colonel Albert Boyd and Captain Charles Yeager were returning from an air show in Cleveland, Ohio, in their P-80 Shooting Stars. One at a time, the pilots "floated" their P-80s to a perfect touchdown.

Years later, William R. Lundgren would report in his book *Across the High Frontier* that Yeager just couldn't resist a wisecrack. Switching on his microphone, Yeager said, "Pretty good, for an old man." He switched his mike off quickly and grinned to himself.

Boyd heard the remark. He snapped back, "Who said that? Get that pilot's name!" Nobody answered, but Boyd must have had little doubt whose West Virginia drawl had come through his headphones.

At 41, Boyd was hardly an old man, and he hardly needed Yeager's opinion on his flying ability. Just recently, on June 19, he had set a new world speed record at low altitude over a course of three kilometers (about two miles). In a white, specially streamlined P-80R, Boyd had reached 623.738 miles per hour, flying less than two hundred feet above a dry lake bed at Muroc Field in California. At that speed and altitude, the slightest mistake could have sent him crashing to his death.

If Boyd knew that Yeager was responsible for the "old man" remark, he decided not to punish him for it. But Yeager wasn't sure what he was in for a few days later when he was told to report to Boyd's office.

After standing at attention for an hour while Boyd lectured and questioned, Yeager knew he wasn't in trouble. Instead, Boyd had summoned Yeager to ask him if he were interested in making a run at the sound barrier. It was dangerous, he warned Yeager; many thought it was impossible.

Yeager was no scientist, but he had a feeling that the sound barrier was a myth. As a child back in Hamlin, he had sometimes come upon old rifle bullets he had fired. Rifle bullets traveled faster than sound, but the bullets Yeager found never looked distorted or damaged from piercing the sound barrier. As it turned out, Yeager would be flying the closest thing to a bullet.

After Bell Aircraft signed a contract with the Army in 1944 to build a supersonic airplane, it quickly learned that nobody knew what shape a supersonic airplane should have. Robert Woods, chief designer for the project, decided to use the .50-caliber machine gun bullet for a model, simply because that bullet was known to travel faster than sound.

That was how the X-1 got its basic shape. Of course, it would not be just like a bullet. For one thing, the X-1 would be hollow, filled with dangerous rocket fuel and a pilot. It would have wings, a tail, and control surfaces. Woods decided that the wings should be short and straight. He made them thin to reduce the effect of supersonic airflow over the tops of the wings, and he placed the elevators high on the tail to keep them out of the turbulence that spilled off the wings in transonic flight. Finally, he made everything unusually strong to withstand whatever forces the airplane might meet.

The contract called for three X-1s. Each had slight differences, such as the thickness of its wings and elevators. The Army would fly the X-1s in a joint research program with a civilian agency, the National Advisory Committee on Aeronautics (NACA).

The first X-1 began flight tests without an engine at Pinecastle Air Base, Florida, in January 1946. A civilian test pilot for Bell, Jack Woolams, flew it first. After dropping in the X-1 from a B-29, he would glide it back to base. This was a way to find out how the airplane handled without the weight and danger of rocket fuel.

The airplane was grounded while the rocket engine was installed then moved to Muroc for powered tests in September. Woolams would not be the pilot, though. While the X-1 was being fitted with its rocket engine, he was killed in August while practicing for a race in a P-39.

The new pilot was Chalmers "Slick" Goodlin. He began making powered flights in the X-1 on December 9, 1946. With each flight he increased its speed a little.

The speed of sound is known as Mach 1. It is named after Ernst Mach, an Austrian physicist who lived from 1838 to

59

1916. He studied the movement of high-speed objects in the air and developed a way to measure speed in terms of the speed of sound. This was important because the speed of sound changes according to atmospheric conditions. At sea level, Mach 1 is about 750 miles per hour; at forty thousand feet, it's about 660 miles per hour.

Instead of a gauge that measured its speed in miles per hour, the X-1 had a special meter called a Machmeter. At any altitude, the Machmeter would show how fast the X-1 was flying compared to the speed of sound. Before the Army would accept the X-1, Bell had to prove that its rocket plane could fly at least eight-tenths the speed of sound, or .8 Mach on the meter. Slick Goodlin reached .8 Mach by the end of January 1947, at an altitude of thirty-five thousand feet.

In the meantime, Yeager progressed from assistant maintenance officer to test pilot. Boyd had watched him fly and had noticed his control and precision. Finally, he had invited Yeager to enroll in the flight-test division's new Flight Performance School.

It was the first school that the Army ever conducted just to train test pilots. It had started in September 1944; Yeager's classes began in January 1946 and finished six months later.

After graduation, he began testing aircraft and flying at air shows. Some of the airplanes he tested were German and Japanese aircraft, brought to Wright Field at the end of the war. He even tested an Me-262, a German jet fighter like the one he had shot down during the war.

He had heard about the X-1. He had seen it occasionally on quick trips to Muroc. Rocket plane, friends had told him. Six thousand pounds of thrust . . . built to go twice the speed of sound . . . some high-paid civilian pilot was going to punch it through the barrier.

Then, in the spring of 1947, the story changed. Slick Goodlin wanted a new contract with Bell. To fly the X-1 against the dreaded sound barrier, he wanted a bonus—$150,000.

While the haggling went on, Boyd grew impatient. It essentially was an Army project, and he wanted to get on with it. He was in charge of the project as head of the flight-test division, although NACA also was taking part. Bell had supplied the test pilot so far, but Boyd would just as soon have an Air Corps pilot be first through the sonic wall.

In May, Boyd called a meeting of Wright Field's test pilots. Who wanted to fly the X-1? he asked. Less than a dozen hands went up. Among the volunteers were Jackie L. Ridley, an aeronautical engineer; Robert Hoover, a dogfight-loving pilot; and Yeager.

Boyd faced a difficult choice. He knew those test pilots well, and he believed that Yeager was the best one for the job. He had watched him fly airplanes with fantastic precision and had seen him keep his cool in dangerous situations. He seemed to have an instinctive feel for airplanes.

On the other hand, the twenty-four-year-old captain was married and had two children, Donald and Mickey. Was it fair to ask a man to take an assignment that might well leave his children without a father, a mission that might end against an invisible wall of deadly forces? As a military test pilot, Yeager would get no fat bonus for the danger, just his captain's salary and flight pay, which amounted to less than $3,400 a year. In exchange, he would get a chance to fly the world's hottest airplane and his name would go into the history books—if he succeeded.

That was one of the questions the colonel put to Yeager when he called him into his office in July. Yeager had an answer: as a husband and father, he would be more careful than ever not to get himself killed.

Boyd had more questions. Who would Yeager want for a backup pilot? Yeager had two recommendations, Ridley and Hoover. Ridley was an engineer and would be able to help Yeager with the technical parts of the project. Hoover was a great pilot and someone whom Yeager knew he could count on.

Boyd sent all three to the Bell Aircraft plant in Buffalo, New York. There, they saw one of the X-1s. They fired its rocket engines and clapped their hands over their ears when it roared and shot out flames. Larry Bell and the design team briefed them on the airplane and explained how it worked.

Then they flew back to Wright Field. Boyd told them that the project was theirs. Yeager would be the pilot.

Chapter 9

GLAMOROUS GLENNIS

His assignment to Muroc put Yeager back together with Glennis and their two children. But their living arrangements on the barren desert near the air base were less than ideal.

The Army had assigned Yeager to Muroc on temporary duty. Officers on temporary duty lacked some of the privileges of officers on regular duty. For example, Yeager's wife and children were not allowed to use the base hospital or to live in base housing. But they decided not to live apart any longer—a wise idea since Yeager's "temporary" duty lasted for several years.

They rented a house on a ranch about thirty miles from the base. The nearest town was twenty miles away. They had only one car, so Glennis often drove her husband to the air base so she would have the car for the day.

Yeager didn't need the car; he was back in school. It was X-1 school, and he was one of only two students. The other was Bob Hoover, his backup pilot.

Their teacher was Dick Frost, the X-1 project engineer from Bell Aircraft. He had been involved in the project from the beginning and had worked with Slick Goodlin during his flights.

The X-1, he assured Yeager and Hoover, was different from anything they had ever flown. Fully loaded with five thousand pounds of alcohol and supercold liquid oxygen, it would drop like a bomb when the B-29 let it go. And a bomb it might be: if its rockets didn't fire, it would plummet to earth and blow a crater in the desert. The only thing to do if the rockets failed would be to dump the fuel load. Even if the plane could glide to a landing under all that weight, the landing gear would collapse and the fuel tanks would rupture. The result would be the same: a big hole in the ground.

There were countless ways for things to go wrong, Frost told them. The airplane was a complicated machine and completely experimental. Yeager learned all that he could about the X-1. He figured that the more he knew, the better his chances would be of surviving an emergency.

Glennis knew a little about the X-1, but when she saw the orange rocket plane for the first time, she was surprised. On the nose were the words "Glamorous Glennis." Yeager had christened the airplane without approval, but nobody dared to change it. *Glamorous Glennis* was his good-luck charm, and in this airplane he would need all the luck he could get.

He began flying the X-1 in the middle of August. He flew it as a glider for the first several flights, without any fuel on board. That was the safest way to learn how the airplane behaved.

On Yeager's first flight, as on every flight, the X-1 was towed to a cross-shaped trench near the runway. The trench just had room for the airplane's body and wings. When the

64

X-1 was ready, the B-29 that would carry it was towed over the trench until the big plane's open bomb bay was directly above it. The small airplane was raised up until it was halfway inside the mother ship's bomb bay. Then it was shackled to the airplane just like a bomb. With the X-1 secured, Yeager, Ridley, and the B-29 crew climbed into the bomber.

For safety reasons, Yeager never entered the X-1 until it was several thousand feet above the ground. The B-29's top speed was only 180 miles per hour when it was climbing. But the X-1 stalled at 190 miles per hour when it was empty and at 240 miles per hour when fully loaded. If anything went wrong and the X-1 fell away or had to be dropped at that speed, it would pitch nose-down and go into a spin. It would fall thousands of feet before a pilot could pull it out of its dive.

Well after takeoff, Yeager went into the bomb bay where the X-1 waited. There was a gloomy darkness in the bay, but the B-29's four big propeller engines filled it with frigid wind and noise. Half the orange airplane's body protruded into the bay, including the canopy.

The cockpit door was low on the right side of the airplane, exposed to the screaming wind underneath the B-29. The way to the cockpit, the only way, was on a ladder that slid down from the bomb bay. Yeager got on the ladder and rode it down. Beneath his feet were thousands of feet of open sky and the brown desert. The freezing wind tried to pry him loose. He held on tightly and, feetfirst, climbed into the cockpit.

Ridley followed him down the ladder to secure the door. The door came down on a cable. Ridley pushed the door against the hatch, and Yeager swung a lever that locked it.

Once in the cockpit, he retrieved the helmet and oxygen mask he had stowed there earlier. He put them on and plugged in his microphone. Then he went through his checklist, making sure that everything he would need for this unpowered flight was ready: radio (to Cardenas: "How do you read me?" Answer: "Loud and clear."); cabin pressure (OK); emergency oxygen bottle (full); landing gear (up, where it was supposed to be). Then he sat in the cockpit, a dark place inside the B-29's bomb bay, and waited.

Flying P-80 jets, Dick Frost and Bob Hoover raced to get in position. They would be the "chase" pilots, following the X-1 to watch its performance and to look for problems that the X-1 pilot might not notice.

The B-29 pilot, Major Bob Cardenas, steered the bomber in a wide circle as it climbed. He needed to keep the dry lake beds within the X-1's gliding range. At twenty-five thousand feet he pitched the bomber into a shallow dive, speeding up to 240 miles per hour. He counted down the seconds, then released the X-1.

Yeager heard a sharp noise and felt a jolt as the shackle unlocked. The airplane fell free, and bright sunlight flooded the cockpit. The X-1 pitched down, but Yeager had it under control. It was a wonderful machine to fly. Without its engines firing, the X-1 made no noise. Happily, Yeager put the airplane through two graceful rolls.

As a glider, the X-1 flew with remarkable stability. On his second flight, Yeager surprised Dick Frost by flying with both hands off the control wheel. Frost was flying chase in a Shooting Star. When he looked into the X-1's cockpit, he saw Yeager with his hands in the air and his feet on the instrument panel. On his third and final unpowered flight, Yeager went after Hoover, playfully dogfighting with him all the way back to the lake bed.

As a glider, the X-1 was fun to fly. Now it was time to fuel it, fire its rockets, and learn the orange beast's true nature.

Major Charles E. Yeager and Major Arthur Murray with the X-1A plane. The X-1A was a rocket-powered plane that reached the speed of Mach 2.5 and an altitude of over ninety thousand feet.

Yeager flew the X-1 research plane (above) to break the sound barrier and the Shooting Star (below), the first U.S. jet fighter to be produced for regular duty.

William R. Enyart presents the Gold Medal of the Federation Aeronautique Internationale to Chuck Yeager in 1949. Yeager's wife Glennis is on his left.

After being assigned to duty in Germany in 1955, Yeager brushes up on his German.

Other planes Yeager enjoyed flying are the F-104 (above) in 1977 and the Tigershark (below) in 1982.

Yeager attends the 1985 Paris Air Show. He ended his flying career with more than ten thousand hours of flying time in some 180 different aircraft.

The X-1, the plane Yeager flew to break the sound barrier, was carried aloft in the B-29's bomb bay. The B-29 climbed to twenty-five thousand feet and then went into a shallow dive before releasing the X-1.

Chapter 10

ROCKET PILOT

On the morning of August 29, the B-29 lumbered into the sky with the fully fueled X-1 nestled underneath. Yeager and the rest of the team followed the usual routine. While the bomber climbed into the sky, Yeager climbed into the X-1 and began going through the checklist.

The checklist was longer this time. It included all the valves, switches, buttons, and gauges that had to do with the rocket engine and fuel.

And the cockpit was *cold*. The liquid oxygen tank was directly behind Yeager, and its intense cold spread slowly through him. The X-1 wasn't made for comfort: it had no cockpit heater, no windshield defroster. Yeager clapped his gloved hands to keep them from turning numb while he waited for the drop. It was a tense wait, like waiting for a bomb to go off, and he was riding in the bomb.

The flight plan was fresh in Yeager's mind. The idea was to take it easy, to go a little faster than Slick Goodlin had gone, but not much. Goodlin had taken the X-1 to .8 Mach. Yeager was to take it to no more than .82 Mach. This was a research aircraft, after all. The airplane carried five hundred pounds of test instruments to gather flight data. NACA's researchers would study the data from this flight, then decide how high and how fast to go next time. That was the best way to do research: one step at a time, studying all the data from the first step before taking the next.

Research aside, Yeager was taking risks. Nobody knew when the X-1 would begin to shudder from transonic forces. Nobody knew whether, at some point above .8 Mach, it would suddenly pitch into a deadly dive. The only sane thing to do was to try to make the risks smaller by taking small steps, a small fraction of a Mach at a time. So the speed limit for this flight was .82 Mach.

Finally, it was five minutes to drop. Yeager pushed his anxiety away and got busy. He brought up the pressures in the alcohol and liquid-oxygen tanks. He checked the fuel dumping systems. He brought up power on the flight instruments. He checked on the chase planes: Dick Frost was behind him, Bob Hoover ahead and high above at forty thousand feet.

The final countdown came, the X-1 dropped, and Yeager lit the first chamber. Sudden acceleration shoved him back in his seat. The orange rocket plane leaped skyward. Hoover's Shooting Star appeared above and fell below as Yeager fired first one chamber, then another. In one wild rush he reached forty-five thousand feet.

The sky turned deep blue, then twilight purple. The sun was brighter than ever, but the stars came out. He was above most of the atmosphere, and there was nothing to diffuse the sunlight and blot out the stars.

What a ride! Yeager did a slow, happy roll. It wasn't in the flight plan, but he didn't care. This was one fantastic flying machine. The rocket plane's short wings cut lazy arcs through the air until Yeager was upside down in a zero-gravity condition. His weight seemed to disappear. Then the chambers fell silent. The zero-G roll had interrupted the fuel flow. He brought the X-1 back to level flight and felt relief when the chambers fired again.

He shut off the engine and nosed over. His skyrocket ride had used only half his fuel. The flight plan called for him to jettison what was left and to glide home. But . . . but . . . this was too much fun. Forget the flight plan! Yeager pushed the X-1 into a dive. He streaked earthward at .8 Mach, silently diving faster than most jets could go at full throttle.

He leveled out below five thousand feet. The ground itself at the high desert base was twenty-three hundred feet. He soared silently into the landing pattern and zipped across the base just a few hundred feet above the runway.

When he passed the control tower, he lit the rockets, all four chambers, all at once. Flames shot out the rear, and the X-1 blasted away from the base. Yeager pulled back on the stick, trying to control the X-1's wild acceleration by steepening the climb. In moments he was going almost straight up, still gaining speed.

The fuel ran out in one minute, but by then he was doing .85 Mach at thirty-five thousand feet. It was the wildest ride Yeager had ever taken, and the thrill of the X-1's incredible speed and power left him giddy. And he had left Slick Goodlin's X-1 speed record in the dust.

Not so giddy when he learned of the flight was Colonel Albert Boyd. From his office at Wright Field, Boyd sent Yeager a terse warning about his departure from the flight plan. Not only had he rolled the X-1, buzzed the base, and fired all four chambers at once, but he had exceeded the flight plan's .82 Mach speed limit. The speed he had reached was truly the edge of the unknown because even wind tunnels in 1947 reached their limit at about .85 Mach.

Boyd could understand a pilot's urge to pull out all the stops and to take the X-1 right to its limit. He could understand the desire to smash the X-1's earlier speed record. But this was an important project. There was no room in it for joyriding. He demanded a personal explanation of Yeager's actions and reminded him, "The Air Force does not consider either you or the plane expendable, so please approach higher speeds progressively and safely to the limit of your best judgment." Yeager promised to follow the rules from then on, and he did.

The flights became less adventuresome but no less dangerous. As the X-1 crept toward the sound barrier, Yeager could feel things happening.

The airplane began buffeting from shock-wave turbulence on Yeager's sixth powered flight. At .86 Mach, his right wing dipped and his controls grew sluggish. At .88 Mach, he looked out at the wing and saw the aileron fluttering.

The buffeting grew worse as the speed increased. As each flight went faster, it became harder to keep the airplane level. The nose wanted to pitch down, then up. When Yeager reached .94 Mach, he suddenly lost elevator control. He pulled back on the control wheel, but the airplane didn't move. He was going about 620 miles per hour with no pitch control. Yeager shut off the rocket engine, dumped out his fuel, and glided back to base.

It looked like they were through. How could he survive in an airplane he couldn't control? The NACA team went over the flight data and concluded that the culprit was a shock wave. At .94 Mach, the shock wave on the tail was right on the elevator hinge line. That canceled anything the pilot tried to do. Knowing what the problem was didn't solve it, though. Even Boyd seemed ready to give up.

There was one chance. The X-1's horizontal stabilizer—the flat, winglike part of the tail—had been built with a pivot. Bell had designed it that way just in case shock waves posed a problem for the elevator. If the elevator went dead, a pilot could use a switch in the cockpit to tilt the stabilizer slightly up or down, using the whole surface as an elevator.

There were some doubts that the stabilizer would work at near-Mach speeds. One of the motors that turned it might stick with the stabilizer in a bad position. The turbulent airflow might grip the stabilizer and keep it from moving or perhaps tear the stabilizer right off the tail. There was only one way to find out.

On Thursday, October 10, Yeager pushed the X-1 back up to Mach .94. As he accelerated, he tested the stabilizer control at several speeds. It worked. Yeager pushed on past the previous limit until his Machmeter read .96 at forty-three thousand feet.

As Yeager and the other researchers learned later, flight data showed that the X-1 had reached .997 Mach on that flight. There was even a chance that he had touched the sound barrier, but the data didn't prove it and no one had heard the expected sonic boom. A sonic boom is the sound of a shock wave sweeping across the earth behind the airplane, following it like the wake of a speedboat. It was expected, but nobody in an airplane had made one, including Yeager on this flight.

Yeager was able to control his pitch, but he had another problem on this flight. Just as he was ending the powered part of the flight, his windshield turned snowy white. The cockpit was so cold that the moisture in the air was freezing on the inside of the windshield. With no windshield defroster, Yeager could use only his hands to clear it off. He tried to wipe it away with his gloves, but it didn't help. He took off his gloves and scraped with his fingernails; no good.

It wasn't a pleasant situation. Visibility out the windshield wasn't good to start with because it followed the curve of the airplane's body. Now he had no view at all. He would have to glide back to the lake bed from forty-three thousand feet, line up correctly, and make a good landing. With no power to go back up, he only had one chance.

He didn't consider bailing out. The X-1 had no ejection seat. Yeager wore a parachute, but the door was just a few feet in front of one of the X-1's knife-edged wings. If Yeager tried to jump, he stood a good chance of being slammed by that wing and cut in half.

He reported his trouble. "I'll talk you down," Frost radioed. Yeager made his way back to base, watching his instruments and listening to Frost's coaching. As he approached the dry lake bed, Frost flew right beside him and radioed landing instructions. The X-1 sank lower, slowing down until it was close to stall speed. Its wheels touched, and the rocket plane settled down without a bounce. Frost landed beside it.

Yeager felt confident once more in his ability to control the X-1 right up to the sound barrier. But something had to be done about that windshield icing. The answer was shampoo. A thin, clear film of shampoo wiped on the windshield kept moisture from condensing.

The NACA team decided that Yeager should try for .97 Mach on his next flight. The next flight would be Tuesday, October 14. He would have the weekend to relax.

On Sunday, Chuck and Glennis Yeager went out for dinner. They went where all the test pilots at Muroc went, to a combination restaurant, bar, motel, riding ranch, and airstrip called Pancho's Fly Inn. It was a place where you could see your friends, eat dinner, have a few drinks, and go horseback riding in the cool night air. That's just what the Yeager's did.

They were coming back to the ranch when they decided to race to the corral. Chuck won, but the prize was a nasty toss over the gate. In the darkness, he didn't see that someone had closed it. He rode his horse right into it. Glennis found him lying in a daze. He felt a sharp, jabbing pain in his right side—a broken rib, Glennis told him.

He needed to see a doctor, but he refused to go to the base hospital. The flight surgeon would ground him. On Monday, Glennis drove him to a local physician in Rosemond. He had two cracked ribs, the doctor informed him. He taped his side, which eased the pain but still left him stiff and sore.

Yeager didn't want to delay the flight schedule. He didn't want Boyd to learn that he had gotten himself thrown off a horse in the dark, and he didn't want to give up his seat in the X-1 to another pilot, not even to Bob Hoover.

He thought about it, then quietly talked to Ridley. He couldn't reach very well with his cracked ribs, but he didn't need to. The most important switches were at his fingertips on the control wheel. Ridley sawed off a broom handle for Yeager to use as a lever when he locked the latch. Yeager tried it and it worked. He stowed the broom handle in the cockpit with his helmet and oxygen mask.

Glennis drove her husband to the base at 6 A.M. on Tuesday. Hoover and others had heard about his spill over Pancho's corral gate. They presented him with a paper bag. Inside it were a carrot, a pair of glasses, and a length of rope. The carrot and glasses were to improve his night vision. They suggested that Yeager could use the rope to tie himself to his horse. They didn't know about his cracked ribs.

Despite his injuries, this flight was routine compared to

last time. The countdown came and the X-1 dropped. Yeager lit the chambers in rapid sequence. He climbed quickly away from the B-29.

At .88 Mach, he felt the airplane begin to buffet. He changed the stabilizer setting, and the buffeting stopped. He shut off two chambers at thirty-six thousand feet, but the X-1 still had plenty of thrust: the air was thinner, giving less resistance, and the fuel load was getting lighter by the second. He was still climbing when he reached .92 Mach at forty thousand feet. He leveled off at forty-two thousand feet and relit a third chamber. The airplane lunged ahead. The Machmeter registered .96 Mach. Yeager was closer than ever to the sonic wall . . . the brick wall in the sky . . . the sound barrier—if it was there.

But something interesting was happening. After the buffeting and the pitching tendencies at lower speeds, the ride was getting *smoother*. "Say, Ridley, make a note here," he radioed. "Elevator effectiveness regained."

The flying was smoother, but the Machmeter was acting up. At .96 Mach it began to fluctuate, the needle bouncing erratically. He reached .965 Mach, then the needle suddenly jumped off the scale, past Mach 1. Yeager felt a thrill, but he radioed calmly, "Ridley, make another note. This Machmeter is acting screwy. It just went off the scale on me."

Down on the desert, a NACA team was tracking Yeager in a radar truck. Suddenly, they heard a distant rumble. Thunder? On a clear day? Son, that was a sonic boom! They radioed the news to Yeager and the others in the air.

Yeager cruised with the meter pegged at Mach 1 for twenty seconds, then shut off the engine. He still had about thirty percent of his fuel left. He dumped it and began his glide back to base.

There was no gaping hole in the desert sky, and no lightly falling dust from shattered bricks. There was only Yeager in the X-1, an orange glider still in one piece, dropping silently back toward Muroc. The dreaded sound barrier was a bump on the Machmeter.

It was a fitting event for the old Army Air Corps. Just a month before Yeager broke the sound barrier, the Army's air arm had begun operating as a separate branch of the military service. Yeager was now in the United States Air Force.

Chapter 11

FAME, BUT NOT FORTUNE

"CONFIDENTIAL PRIORITY. XS-1 BROKE MACH NO. ONE AT 42000 FT ALT. CONDITIONS IMPROVED WITH INCREASE OF AIRSPEED. DATA BEING REDUCED AND WILL BE FORWARDED WHEN COMPLETED. END."

That was the message that sped from Muroc in California to Wright Field in Ohio. Muroc base commander Colonel Sigma Gilkey telegraphed the information immediately after the flight.

As it turned out, Gilkey's was one of the few messages about Yeager's accomplishment that escaped the desert air base. The Air Force decided that the news was too valuable to release. Chuck Yeager had made one of the most important flights in history, a feat that should have earned him fame, if not fortune. But the fame would be slow in coming.

That didn't bother Yeager. He flew because he wanted to fly. He flew dangerous assignments for the Air Force because it was his duty. He didn't seek fame; if anything, he tended to be close-mouthed about his work. He didn't even tell Glennis about breaking Mach 1 when she came to pick him up. He just flopped into the seat beside her.

Glennis had seen the white contrail of her husband's dash

across the sky, but she had not heard the sonic boom. Only when Dick Frost and Bob Hoover ran up and began shouting and thumping his back did she learn that her husband had just made one of the most important flights in history.

Yeager's friends dragged him back out of the car. They celebrated over lunch and drinks in the officer's club. They were noisy and happy; anyone in the club must have realized that some breakthrough had taken place. Since this was the X-1 team, it could not have been hard to guess what the breakthrough was.

But Boyd soon put a damper on the festivities. From Washington had come the order to keep the news of Yeager's flight under tight security. Boyd forwarded the order to Muroc just as the X-1 team was making plans for a big party at Pancho's. Reluctantly, they canceled their plans and went to the Yeagers' home instead.

Yeager's flight in the X-1 might be described as his second most dangerous ride that day. Well into a night of drinking, the pain in his side apparently deadened by alcohol, Yeager decided to go for a motorcycle ride on the desert. He raced through the darkness with the headlight off, leaving a trail of dust through the brush and the Joshua trees. His none-too-sober friends followed as best they could in a car. He lost control once and slid on his side across a dirt road. But he jumped up, laughed, and took off again. Eventually, he got back to his home and went on with the party.

While the X-1 team celebrated privately, the public heard nothing about Yeager's flight. Word finally got out late in

December, when *Aviation Week* magazine broke the story. That caused a flurry of newspaper reports. "Information concerning his super-sonic flight was disclosed by *Aviation Week* magazine, although government sources have made no official disclosures," reported the *Herald-Dispatch* back in Huntington, West Virginia.

The Air Force doggedly stuck to its rule on silence. In fact, the Air Force asked the U.S. Justice Department to investigate whether *Aviation Week*'s announcement violated national security. The department concluded that it had broken no law.

On June 10, 1948, Secretary of the Air Force Stuart Symington finally admitted what everybody already knew. By then, Yeager had flown the X-1 past the sound barrier several times. NACA matched the Air Force announcement by revealing that two of its test pilots, Herbert B. Hoover and the late Howard Lilly, also had flown faster than sound in the second X-1. (Lilly had died on May 3, 1948, while testing another experimental supersonic airplane, the Douglas Skystreak.)

Yeager was finally getting the recognition he had earned. On June 15, he received the Mackay Trophy from General Hoyt S. Vandenberg, Air Force Chief of Staff. The trophy was for the outstanding military flight of the year.

On December 17, 1948, the forty-fifth anniversary of the Wright brothers' first flight, President Harry S. Truman presented him with the Collier Trophy, which is one of aviation's top trophies. The annual award was started in 1911 by

Robert J. Collier, a pilot and the publisher of *Collier's Weekly*. Yeager shared the award with Bell Aircraft president Larry Bell for his work in producing the X-1 and with John Stack, a NACA engineer who had helped design the X-1. (Stack later shared in the 1951 Collier Trophy for helping to overcome the problem of studying transonic speeds in wind tunnels.)

Yeager soon began receiving all kinds of recognition. At a banquet in Dayton, the International Aviation Federation honored him with a gold medal. The University of West Virginia awarded him an honorary doctor of science degree in 1948. Marshall University in Huntington, West Virginia, awarded him with an honorary doctor of science degree in 1969. The National Aviation Hall of Fame in Dayton added him to its roster of air pioneers in 1973.

Time magazine featured him on the cover of its April 18, 1949, edition and carried a detailed story about his flight "through the dreaded 'sonic wall.'" By then, Yeager was used to penetrating the mythical wall of sound. In the *Time* magazine article he joked, "We've punched so many holes in that old wall, you can see 'em all over the Mojave."

He earned another medal when he pushed the speed frontier to nearly two and a half times the speed of sound in 1953. The following year, President Dwight D. Eisenhower presented him with the Harmon International Trophy. This was the same Eisenhower who, ten years earlier, had granted Yeager's wish to return to combat after his escape from France in World War II.

One honor for which he didn't qualify was the Congressional Medal of Honor. This was the highest honor a citizen could receive for actions to help the country in wartime, but Yeager had made his supersonic flight during peacetime. Many of his friends felt that he deserved it anyway. They asked members of Congress to make an exception. In December of 1975, twenty-eight years after the flight and nine months after his retirement from the Air Force, Congress passed a special law to give Yeager a "silver medal, equivalent to a noncombat Medal of Honor." President Gerald R. Ford presented him with the Congressional Silver Medal in 1976.

That wasn't his last medal from a president. In 1985, President Ronald Reagan included Yeager in a list of thirteen individuals to receive the Presidential Medal of Freedom, the nation's highest civilian award.

Through it all, Yeager kept his low-key attitude. "I had a job to do and I did it," he said in one Associated Press story. In another, he said that flying through the sound barrier was "no different than sitting in your armchair at home."

As usual, he let his airplanes do his talking. In October of 1948, he flew a Shooting Star jet fighter under the South Side Bridge in Charleston, West Virginia's capital city. He was flying in an air show, but zooming under a downtown bridge was not in the program.

Paul Bowles had returned to Charleston to become a lawyer after flying with Yeager in World War II. He didn't see Yeager fly under the bridge, but he heard all about it soon afterward. He said that Yeager banked through a turn and "got down on the river pretty low. . . . What he didn't know was that there was some kind of regatta on the river."

Roaring toward the bridge at jet speed, Yeager's sudden appearance caught the people in the boats by surprise. "People were jumping out of the boats left and right," Bowles said. "He's better known for that in the Charleston area than for breaking the sound barrier."

Yeager became a showpiece for the Air Force. He spoke at banquets and public events all over the country. Throughout his career, he emphasized how important the Air Force was in his life.

But the Air Force was slow in giving Yeager the kind of rewards that would help his family. It kept him on "temporary" duty at Muroc for two years. During that time his family wasn't allowed to use the base hospital. Glennis had to deliver their third child, Sharon, in a fourteen-bed hospital in the town of Mojave. The Air Force didn't promote him to major until February 15, 1951, more than three years after his first supersonic flight. It was his first step up in rank since his promotion to captain in October 1944.

The Air Force also refused to let him profit from his fame. His superiors denied him permission to sign contracts that would have brought him nice sums of money for the rights to make a flim about his life. Years later, when seven military pilots were chosen to be the nation's first astronauts, they were permitted to sign big contracts with *Life* magazine for their life stories.

Chapter 12

NEW SPEEDS FOR A NEW ERA

With the myth of the sound barrier put to rest, aviation researchers made rapid progress in supersonic flight through the rest of the 1940s and 1950s. Both the Air Force and the Navy were working on faster-than-sound projects with NACA. Both were ordering a number of different designs for supersonic aircraft.

By the time World War II ended, the United States had built up the world's strongest air power. U.S. military leaders wanted to make sure it stayed that way. As soon as Chuck Yeager proved that airplanes could fly faster than sound, supersonic warplanes went into production.

On April 26, 1948, North American Aviation test pilot George "Wheaties" Welch nosed one of his company's new F-86 fighters into a shallow dive and reached Mach 1. It was just six months after Yeager's first supersonic flight. The F-86 Sabre Jet was the first supersonic airplane to go into regular service. The Sabre Jet made its fame in the Korean conflict in the early 1950s, knocking the Soviet Union's new MiG-15 jet fighter out of the sky by the hundreds.

Military and NACA researchers were hard pressed to stay ahead of the industry. Airplane companies were making plans for jet fighters and bombers that could pass Mach

1 and Mach 2 in level flight, but there wasn't enough research data to be sure how well these designs would work.

While Yeager continued to fly the X-1, other supersonic research ships were in the works. Advanced versions of the X-1, swept-wing jets and rockets, and even more exotic designs were headed for Muroc.

Test pilots at Muroc competed for the hottest airplanes and the fastest flights, and more test pilots seemed to arrive every day. The Air Force moved its flight-test division from Wright Field to Muroc in 1951. (By then, Albert Boyd was a general, and Muroc had been renamed Edwards Air Force Base. Its new name was in memory of Glenn Edwards, an Air Force test pilot who had died in a crash there.)

Yeager was among the best of the test pilots at Edwards. Although each test pilot likes to think that he is the best, some were willing to say that Yeager was better. Frank K. "Pete" Everest, Jr., in his autobiography *Fastest Man Alive*, bluntly called Yeager "the best test pilot in the world." Some pilots, like Everest, admired his ability. Some disliked him for his fame, but nobody could deny that he kept raising the bid for the fastest flight.

But high speed meant high risks, and the orange X-1 seemed to grow more dangerous with each flight. The troubles started on his first X-1 flight after breaking the sound barrier, on October 27. When the B-29 released Yeager, he dropped like a stone, silent and powerless. A faulty main battery switch prevented him from firing his engines and using the radio.

He was falling faster every second in an airplane loaded with fuel. He had to do something, fast. Reaching behind him, he turned an emergency valve that would dump out the fuel. It began spewing out of the X-1 as the silent rocket plane dropped. He turned into his final landing approach, still not knowing whether he had dumped out enough fuel to land safely. Only the landing itself would tell.

He held off his landing until the last moment to give that valve more time to dump fuel. The X-1 swept over the lake bed while Yeager fought to keep it airborne without stalling. Finally, he had to set the plane down. The landing gear held.

After that flight came a series of problems with the bomb shackle, which held the X-1 under the mother ship. When it came time to release the airplane, the shackle would not let go. It was finally decided that the B-29 would have to land with the X-1 still attached. Yeager crawled back out of the orange rocket plane and back into the B-29, hoping that the shackle would not suddenly open while he was halfway out of one airplane and halfway into the other.

Fire was the next threat. In January 1948, Yeager was flying Mach 1.10 at thirty-eight thousand feet when he heard a noise, felt a strange vibration, and saw smoke in the cockpit. He shut off his rockets, dumped his fuel, and glided home. On the next flight, his cockpit filled with dark smoke.

Nothing frightens a pilot more than fire in his airplane. With its tons of explosive fuel, the X-1 was like a huge orange firecracker waiting to be lit. Whenever the fire warning light came on, Yeager had to decide whether to dump his fuel. If the fire was near the fuel lines and had burned through them, dumping the fuel would just feed it to the fire. And every time he flew, it seemed, the fire warning light came on.

Yeager began to dread each X-1 flight. He dreamed about it. Each night the dream was the same. He was trapped inside the cockpit as it filled with flames. He would be trying to bail out, trying to shove that door open, when Glennis would wake him up. He would find himself at their bedroom window, trying to climb out.

After twenty-three powered flights, Colonel Boyd ordered a break in Yeager's routine. Yeager made no protest. Other pilots flew the X-1 past the speed of sound, including Ridley and Boyd, while Yeager flew chase in a Shooting Star. But Yeager continued to fly dangerous missions, sometimes only so that the Air Force could claim a "first."

On January 5, 1949, Yeager took off from the ground in the X-1. There were some who disputed the Air Force's claim to the first supersonic flight because the X-1 never took off from the ground under its own power. Yeager, Larry Bell of Bell Aircraft, and the Air Force grew concerned in 1948 as the Navy prepared to test its own supersonic airplane, the Douglas Skyrocket, with takeoffs from the ground.

The X-1 had not been designed to take off like an ordinary airplane; the landing gear were too weak. After careful calculations, Ridley concluded that the weak landing gear could stand it if the X-1 carried only half a load of fuel. On takeoff, Yeager fired all four rocket chambers at once and blasted into the sky. He reached Mach 1.03 at twenty-three thousand feet in eighty seconds. He landed less than three minutes after takeoff. The Douglas Skyrocket flew many times and produced valuable information, but Yeager had sealed his claim for the first supersonic flight.

The next record was Mach 2, twice the speed of sound. The Air Force had thought it would reach Mach 2 shortly after Yeager's Mach-1 flight, but a series of accidents, which destroyed some research aircraft, delayed the attempt for several years. In late 1953, the Air Force set its sights on December 17, the fiftieth anniversary of the Wright brothers' first powered airplane flight. Hitting Mach 2 a few days ahead of that date would be a great way to observe the anniversary. If Yeager did it, he would be the first man to break both Mach 1 and Mach 2. The payoff to the Air Force in terms of publicity would be enormous. It made plans for Yeager, now a major, to fly the X-1A, a more advanced version of the old X-1.

But the Air Force had competition. A. Scott Crossfield, an aerospace researcher and former NACA test pilot at Edwards, was flying Navy airplanes with Mach-2 potential. In his autobiography *Always Another Dawn*, Crossfield wrote, "The Navy had not the slightest intention of letting the Air Force pluck this plum without a stiff fight."

Crossfield made the first Mach-2 flight in the Navy's Douglas Skyrocket on November 20, 1953. In a shallow dive, he piloted the Skyrocket just past Mach 2 at sixty-two thousand feet. Unlike Yeager's Mach-1 flight, Crossfield's Mach-

2 flight was not kept secret. He became famous overnight, and the Navy shared in the glory. Yeager wanted a chance to give Crossfield's record an unforgettable beating. The Air Force, frustrated at the Navy's victory, was willing to let him try. He thought he could do it before December 17.

He would fly the X-1A. It looked much like the X-1, but it was longer and its cockpit was more like that of a normal jet fighter. Its Machmeter could register up to Mach 3.

It was a risky plan. In his autobiography, Crossfield wrote that he believed the X-1A would become "directionally unstable"—likely to flip end-for-end—at Mach 1.8. Bell Aircraft engineers thought he could reach Mach 2 but warned him not to go past Mach 2.3. Also, the X-1A would fly at altitudes of seventy thousand feet or more, where the air thinned out almost to nothing. The pilot had to wear a special pressure suit in case his cockpit lost pressure.

Worst of all, there was no way to escape from the X-1A in an emergency. Not only did it not have an ejection seat but it had a door that was bolted into place from the outside. Once the door was on, the pilot was locked in for the whole ride.

While Crossfield gave interviews to news reporters about his Mach-2 flight, Yeager practiced in the X-1A. He made three trial flights, taking it to Mach 1.3, Mach 1.5, and Mach 1.9. On the fourth flight, on December 12, he planned to pull out all the stops.

The mother ship carried him to thirty-two thousand feet and dropped him. He fired his rockets and climbed, watching the stars come out as the air thinned. He left his chase team, Jack Ridley and Major Kit Murray, far below. He climbed past sixty thousand feet, past seventy thousand feet, then saw the Machmeter slide steadily past Crossfield's Mach-2 record. Finally, at seventy-four thousand feet, Yeager reached Mach 2.44—1,612 miles per hour.

He had ten seconds to congratulate himself. Then he noticed the X-1A's nose beginning to drift to the left—a slow yaw turn. He tried to nudge the nose back with the right rudder pedal, but the airplane didn't respond. Instead, the right wing began to rise. He was sliding into a rolling cartwheel at more than twice the speed of sound.

The airplane went wild, rolling and spinning at the same time. Savage forces hurled Yeager back and forth against his straps until he was stunned and helpless. His helmet smacked the canopy and cracked it. He heard a whoosh of escaping air and felt his pressure suit inflate. It saved him from the sudden loss of pressure, but it did so by squeezing him painfully until he could hardly breathe. Meanwhile, the X-1A tumbled crazily and fell like a stone toward the Tehachapi mountains below.

At some level almost beneath his awareness, Yeager's years of experience were still at work. Dimly, he tried to analyze the situation and figure out what to do. He had no idea how to bring the airplane out of its frenzied fall, but he worked the controls until the X-1A flipped out of its wild gyrations into a normal spin, a spin that he could handle, even battered and dazed. He stopped the spin at twenty-five thousand feet.

Nobody in the other airplanes or on the ground knew that anything was wrong. He had zoomed out of sight, leaving only a white contrail against the sky. Then they heard a voice on their radios, gasping and fighting to make words. "I'm . . . I'm down . . . I'm down to 25,000 feet over Tehachapi." Everyone knew then that something was terribly wrong. The news stunned everybody. His next words were even more frightening: "Don't know whether I can get back to the base or not."

Ridley radioed: "At 25,000 feet, Chuck?"

Yeager was obviously in pain: "I can't say much more. I got to save myself for the landing . . . I'm . . . Christ!"

Ridley prompted him again, desperate to find out what was happening. "What say, Chuck?"

"I say I don't know if I tore anything up or not but . . . Christ!"

He was somewhere in the sky, fighting for his life. But where? Murray pleaded, "Tell us where you are if you can."

But as quickly as things had gone haywire, Yeager's voice became calm again. He had the airplane under control. Gliding back toward base, he was beginning to believe he would live. "I think I can get back to the base OK, Jack.

"Boy, I'm not going to do that any more."

Chapter 13

BACK TO THE JETS

Yeager meant what he said. He never flew the X-1A again. He never flew another rocket plane. At age twenty-nine, he was feeling a need to do something different, a need to get away from the daily dangers of exotic rocket planes and the bitter competition among the test pilots. He was tired of sacrificing his family life, too. He had four children now, two boys and two girls, and sometimes he felt that he hardly knew them.

He wasn't in any mood to give up fast airplanes, though. In his 1961 book *X-15 Diary*, Richard Tregaskis wrote:

> Yeager, who liked the companionship and good fellowship of his World War II fighter out-fit, was weary of being a star performer and prima donna. . . . He missed the camaraderie, the joking, and the pranks, the horsing around. . . . "It's too individualistic," Yeager said. "There's no teamwork, like in a squadron. It's a job for one man. You end up at each other's throats."

But he was not done testing airplanes. Across the Pacific, a North Korean pilot defected to the south in a Russian

MiG-15 fighter. It gave the United States a rare opportunity to examine a Russian airplane and to find out just how advanced it really was.

Yeager got the assignment. He and another test pilot named Tom Collins met the MiG-15 at Kadena Air Force Base on the island of Okinawa in February 1954. General Boyd and a crew of technicians from Wright-Patterson Air Force Base also went to evaluate it.

The weather conditions were terrible. A tropical storm was paying the island an unwelcome visit. The test flights would have to take place in rain, wind, turbulent clouds, and poor visibility, but Yeager put the airplane through every test he could imagine.

From his tests, the United States learned that the MiG-15 could fly higher, climb faster, and accelerate faster than its American counterpart, the F-86 Sabre Jet. But he learned by trying that a MiG pilot could not maintain control of the jet near transonic speed. He tested it by putting the jet into a full-power, straight-down dive from fifty thousand feet. Later, a Russian pilot told him that even they never attempted that in a MiG-15.

His MiG testing marked the end of an eight-year career as a test pilot. Shortly after he returned to Edwards Air Force Base, the Air Force offered him the command of a squadron of Sabre Jets. It was what he had been hoping for.

In October 1954, Yeager returned as a friend to a place where, ten years earlier, he had been fighting as an enemy: Germany. He was assigned to the 417th Fighter Squadron at

Hahn Air Base in West Germany. The base was near Wiesbaden, east of Frankfurt. The pilots had heard about his supersonic flights, and soon he proved that he could outshoot and out-dogfight the best of them. He earned their respect and loyalty.

He was with the squadron at Hahn until April 1956. In March of that year, Major Yeager became Lieutenant Colonel Yeager. In April, the squadron moved to Toul-Rosieres Air Base in France. Yeager returned to the United States in September of 1957, when he was offered command of a squadron of F-100 Super Sabres.

The new assignment put the Yeagers back in the desert at George Air Force Base, not far from Edwards. But the F-100 marked a new age in military aviation, and Yeager wanted to be a part of it.

North American Aviation's F-100 was the first jet fighter that could reach supersonic speed in level flight. It could also refuel during flight from a tanker airplane. Aerial refueling meant that airplanes could fly anywhere without having to land and refuel. In an emergency, the Air Force could send a squadron of fighters from the United States to any foreign country quickly, refueling them over the ocean. Yeager led his F-100 squadron on practice missions to Spain, Italy, and Japan.

By now it seemed that Yeager, who had started out as a country boy with no plans for his life, had done everything but go to college. The Air Force took care of that. In 1960 it sent him to the Air War College at Maxwell Air Force Base in Montgomery, Alabama. He graduated at the top of his class and, in 1961, was promoted to full colonel.

In June 1961, almost eight years after he had left it, Yeager returned to Edwards Air Force Base. This time he was not a test pilot. He was the deputy director, and later director, of the flight-test division. He held that position for little more than a year. In July 1962, the Air Force named him commandant of the Aerospace Research Pilot School.

This school was much different than the one he had attended fifteen years earlier at Wright Field. It was turning out the Air Force's first astronauts. Some graduates of the school went to the National Aeronautics and Space Administration (NASA) to fly Gemini space capsules. Others flew NASA's X-15 rocket plane, which explored the edge of space at Mach 6. Some of them eventually became space-shuttle pilots.

Yeager had flown close to the edge of space in the X-1A, but he was never to have a chance to become an astronaut himself. The Air Force had ambitious plans in the 1950s and early 1960s to develop its own space force. Even before NASA started sending up astronauts in capsules, the Air Force was planning a rocket plane called the X-20 Dyna Soar. It was to be launched by a rocket and landed like an airplane. The Air Force also had plans for a small space station called the Manned Orbiting Laboratory.

Those plans were canceled in the 1960s by President Lyndon Johnson, who wanted to keep outer space free of military forces. But the technology that the Air Force developed for the Dyna Soar eventually went into today's space-shuttle fleet. In the early 1980s, the Air Force created a Space Command and built its own space-shuttle center at Vandenberg Air Force Base in California.

The only chance that Yeager might have had to fly in space in the 1960s would have been as a NASA astronaut in a space capsule. But Yeager, like some other pilots, didn't think riding in a space capsule was really piloting. "In the Mercury capsules, you weren't flying," he said in a 1981 *Washington Post* story. "You were sitting there strapped in with your arms folded. And you didn't land the thing. It fell into the ocean, and you waited for $10 million worth of ship to come rescue you." In fact, NASA's first Mercury "astronaut" was a chimpanzee. Early astronauts were treated more like test subjects who were fired into space than like pilots who flew their own ships.

Still, Yeager had the challenge of developing the first Air Force school to teach pilots how to fly in space. They had specially modified airplanes that could fly to the edge of space, giving the pilots a taste of flight beyond the atmosphere.

The airplane was a Lockheed F-104 Starfighter, a Mach-2 fighter with short, razor-thin wings. Because of its long body, its short wings, and its speed, it came to be known as a "missile with a man in it." Yeager had tested the F-104 in the 1950s, and now the F-104 would test him.

The modified version that Yeager's school used carried a rocket engine to propel it where there was too little air to feed its two jet engines. It had small steering rockets for controlling the airplane when the air became too thin for the plane's control surfaces to work. But it still had the F-104's nasty habit of suddenly pitching its nose up in steep climbs at high speed, then whirling into a flat spin.

Yeager knew about the pitch-up problem from his earlier experience with F-104s. He decided to test the pilot school's models to discover their safety limits. He made two test flights on December 12, 1963, exactly ten years after his terrifying Mach-2 ride in the X-1A.

The morning flight went perfect. He took it up to 108,000 feet in a steep climb. At the top, the plane tried to pitch up, but he controlled it with a steering rocket in the nose of the ship. He repeated his flight in the afternoon, reaching the top of his climb at 104,000 feet. Again the nose pitched up, but this time it refused to come down when he fired the steering rocket.

The F-104 fell into its deadly flat spin, falling like a stone through the desert sky. Its jet engines had lost power and would not light up again. Without power, nothing he could do would bring the airplane out of the spin. Finally, at about fourteen thousand feet, he gave up. Unlike the X-1A, this airplane had an ejection seat. He used it.

A rocket charge under the seat blasted him out of the cockpit. Another charge kicked him free from the seat. He fell through the air, sealed in his oxygen-filled pressure suit, while his parachute streamed out. The ejection seat fell with him, its rocket tube still sputtering flames. As it tumbled, it dribbled fire on his parachute lines. Yeager saw them smoldering and prayed that they wouldn't burn through.

When the parachute popped open, he slowed down with a jerk. The ejection seat didn't. It smashed into him, broke the faceplate of his helmet, gashed his head, and set fire to the collar of his suit. Fed by the pure oxygen in his suit, the fire flared inside the helmet. Choking on hot air and smoke, he managed to shut off the oxygen flow.

He hit the ground and began stripping off his suit. He couldn't see out of his left eye, but it was his hand that hurt. He had touched one of his hands to his helmet and the glove had caught fire.

He was out in the middle of the Mojave Desert, but someone on a nearby highway had spotted him and came running to help. But when he saw Yeager's charred face and saw parts of his fingers come off when he peeled away his burned glove, he turned away, sick to his stomach. A helicopter picked up Yeager and rushed him to the base hospital.

He lost the tips of two fingers, but fortunately, he didn't lose his left eye. The gash from the ejection seat had saved it. "Well, what happened was my eye socket filled up with blood, which caked from the fire and protected my eye," he said in the *Washington Post* story. His wonderful eyesight was intact, but he spent a month in the base hospital undergoing a painful recovery. To keep scars from covering half his face, a physician had to scrape the scar tissue away with a knife every few days.

It was his last military test flight, but it wasn't the end of his flying. Almost two decades after his P-51 days, Yeager went back to war.

Chapter 14

ALWAYS ANOTHER WAR

Strictly speaking, America was not at war. No war had been declared, but U.S. troops were fighting in Vietnam. Vietnam had been split into two nations after World War II. The Soviet Union supported the north, while the United States supported the south. It was a long, bitter war that ended with defeat for South Vietnam after the United States left it on its own. It left Americans divided and angry over whether it had been right to take part in the war.

Such questions didn't bother Yeager in July 1966, when the Air Force assigned him to the 405th Fighter Wing at Clark Air Base in the Philippines. His country told him to go, so he went. His duty as a member of the armed forces was to obey orders. Besides, he was a combat pilot, and here was a chance for combat flying.

He was responsible for squadrons of fighters and bombers stationed in Taiwan, Thailand, the Philippines, and Vietnam. Some of the airplanes under his command carried nuclear weapons, although they were never used. He also flew on combat missions himself—127 altogether—in a B-57 Canberra, a twin-engine bomber. Yeager was one of only a few who fought in both World War II and the war in Vietnam.

He left the Philippines in February 1968, when the Air Force made him commander of the Fourth Tactical Fighter Wing at Seymour Johnson Air Force Base in North Carolina. He led squadrons of F-4 Phantom jets. (The Phantom flies at Mach 2 and carries sixteen thousand pounds of bombs.)

He came close to seeing combat again. On January 28 of that year, North Korea captured a U.S. Navy boat, the *Pueblo*, and imprisoned its crew of eighty-three for more than a year. The Fourth Tactical Fighter Wing was sent to South Korea in case the *Pueblo* crisis turned into a battle. It didn't, but Yeager's wing stayed close by for six months.

During World War II, Chuck Yeager once had to parachute into enemy territory. Now his oldest son, Donald, was doing the same thing in Vietnam, on purpose. He was a paratrooper in the Army's 173rd Airborne Brigade. The Army had drafted him out of college. When Chuck Yeager found himself in South Korea, he managed an occasional secret trip down to Vietnam to visit his son. On some visits he went all the way into the combat-zone camps to see Don with his outfit. Don served his combat tour without injury.

Yeager's Air Force career was winding down, but he still had important assignments to fulfill. He had done well on all his assignments and had established a flawless record in leading fighter squadrons to faraway stations without problems. His service record helped him take his final step up in rank: on August 1, 1969, Colonel Yeager became Brigadier General Yeager.

He was still on the move. In June of that year, he was assigned vice commander of the Seventeenth Air Force at Ramstein Air Base in West Germany. He spent eighteen months there, then eighteen months as U.S. defense representative to Pakistan.

He returned to the United States, and to the California desert, in March 1973. He was special assistant to the commander of the Air Force Inspection and Safety Center at Norton Air Force Base. Three months later, the Air Force named him director of Aerospace Safety.

That assignment helped keep Yeager in the pilot's seat through the end of his career. In most cases, the Air Force does not allow its generals to fly their own airplanes. But it made an exception in his case, bowing to his argument that he could not tell if an airplane was safe unless he flew it.

Yeager served until 1975. Although he was only fifty-two, much younger than most people when they retire, he had served almost thirty-four years in the armed forces. From a raw recruit in 1941 whose only ambition was to fly, Yeager ended his career as an Air Force general with more than ten thousand hours of flying time in some 180 different aircraft.

The end of his military career did not mean the end of his flying. He has continued to fly everything from ultralights to the latest jet fighters. He serves as a consulting test pilot for Northrop, flying its supersonic F-5G and F-20 jet fighters. On October 14, 1982, at age sixty, Yeager celebrated the thirty-fifth anniversary of his supersonic X-1 flight by flying at Mach 1.45 in an F-5G Tigershark.

In recent years, a new generation of Americans has rediscovered Yeager. He has experienced a new wave of publicity, largely because of a book by Tom Wolfe, *The Right Stuff*. The book was about test pilots and the first astronauts, and it described Yeager as the best of all the test pilots, the one with "the right stuff."

This time, Yeager has been free to accept the fortune as well as the fame. When Wolfe's book led to a motion picture with the same name, Yeager served as a consultant and played a small role as a bartender. He also appeared on national television commercials for AC spark plugs and in advertisements for other products and businesses. In 1985, Bantam Books published his autobiography, coauthored by Leo Janos. Simply titled *Yeager*, it was an instant best-seller.

What is the "right stuff"? Yeager has come to be a symbol for the person who always knows what to do . . . the guy who never freezes up or panics in the face of danger . . . the supersonic superhero who knows which button to push or which way to turn at the critical instant . . . the nerveless warrior who describes death in terms of "getting clobbered" or "drilling a hole in the desert." In his book, Tom Wolfe rolled all those characteristics into a general quality he called "the right stuff."

Yeager never planned on becoming a hero. He wanted to fly. He had marvelous eyesight, good coordination, an interest in mechanical things, and a strong competitive spirit. In the things that interested him, he worked hard to be as good as his abilities would allow.

He also had a good measure of luck, from running into helpful French farmers (instead of German troops) when he was shot down in World War II to picking an assignment at Wright Field just as the Air Corps was starting its test-pilot school and X-1 program. But luck only helps those who have the ability and the desire to take advantage of it.

More important than having "the right stuff," Yeager told a *Washington Post* reporter in 1985, was being "in the right place at the right time." Indeed, the history of aviation is such that there were only a few years when someone with Yeager's background could accomplish all that he did. The first airplane flight took place only twenty years before his birth, and the sound barrier fell only twenty-four years after. Had Yeager been born a generation earlier, the world would not have been ready; had he been born a generation later, he would have been too late.

Thirty-five years after he broke the sound barrier, Yeager flew the Tigershark fighter jet. When landed, he said flying the Tigershark was "a piece of cake" compared to the X-1.

Chapter 15

A NEW ERA

The "sonic wall" was a wall between two eras in aviation history. On one side were the Wright brothers and piston engines; on the other were supersonic flight and the edge of space. Chuck Yeager was in the orange rocket plane's cockpit when the time came to blast out of the first era and into the second. With the sonic wall breached, progress in aviation surged ahead.

• In 1948, a North American Aviation Sabre Jet in a dive became the first jet fighter (as opposed to an airplane built solely for research) to exceed Mach 1.

• In 1950, NACA researchers, led by John Stack, developed the transonic wind tunnel, and in 1951 researcher Richard Whitcomb developed an important rule on the proper shapes for supersonic airplanes.

• In 1953, A. Scott Crossfield reached Mach 2 in the Douglas D-558-2 Skyrocket. The same year, a prototype of the first jet that was able to reach Mach 1 in level flight—the North American F-100 Super Sabre—began flying.

• In 1954, the Lockheed F-104 Starfighter, the first jet able to reach Mach 2 in level flight, took to the air.

• In 1956, the first supersonic bomber, the Convair B-58 Hustler, made its first flights. The four-engine, delta-wing jet could carry ten tons of bombs or fuel and had a top speed of Mach 2.5, faster than Yeager had gone just three years earlier in the X-1A.

• In 1962, flight testing began for the Lockheed SR-71 Blackbird, a reconnaissance aircraft able to cruise faster than Mach 3 at altitudes above eighty thousand feet. The first jet aircraft able to reach Mach 3, the Blackbird, set a world speed record of Mach 3.3 (2,193 miles per hour) in 1976. Much about the aircraft remains secret.

• In 1965, two North American XB-70A Valkyries, experimental versions of Mach-3+ bombers, exceeded Mach 3 for the first time. Powered by six jet engines, the 250-ton bombers first flew in 1964. The B-70 was intended to be capable of outrunning enemy aircraft and of dropping nuclear bombs from high altitudes, but it soon became obvious that it could not outrun the latest surface-to-air missiles. The B-70 never went into service.

• In 1967, the General Dynamics F-111, a Mach-2.5 fighter-bomber, entered service. The F-111 featured "swing wings" that could pivot to different angles at different speeds. Still in service, it carries up to 31,500 pounds of bombs.

The next barrier was space itself. In the 1960s, astronauts reached space by riding in capsules atop tall booster rockets. Capsules carried them around the earth and to the moon, but at the end of their missions the capsules dangled under parachutes and dropped into the ocean. The astronauts had to wait for helicopters to ferry them to ships—far more costly, and far less practical, than an airplane alighting on a runway at its home base.

NASA's X-15 rocket plane could not fly as high or as fast as space capsules, but it was close to a winged spaceship. In more than seven hundred research flights, X-15s reached Mach 6.7 (4,520 miles per hour), experienced air-friction temperatures of three thousand degrees, soared to more than 350,000 feet, and landed on runways. Some of the pilots were graduates of Yeager's Aerospace Research Pilot School.

When the time came for the next era in aviation, Yeager was on hand. On April 14, 1981, the first winged spaceship flipped out of orbit and glided to a landing at Edwards Air Force Base.

The Space Shuttle Columbia had been launched by booster rockets from Kennedy Space Center on April 12. Its crew of two included John Young and Robert Crippin, NASA astronauts. During its fifty-four-hour, thirty-six-orbit flight, it had reached an altitude of about 150 miles. Now it was to make the first airplane-style return from space, coasting home just as Yeager had done thirty-three years earlier in *Glamorous Glennis*. Yeager was waiting at Edwards to describe the landing for National Public Radio.

Columbia stopped being a spaceship when its delta-shaped wings touched the atmosphere at four-hundred thousand feet over the Pacific Ocean. Suddenly, it was a glider doing Mach 24. Its nose pitched high, Columbia used the air to slow its descent. The heat of friction surrounded the ship with a pink glow.

It announced its arrival over Edwards with a familiar greeting—a sonic boom. Then Young lined it up for its final approach, lowered its wheels, and landed gently on the dry lake bed.

Yeager described the new era in a few brief words. "It's a beautiful touchdown," he said. "Beautiful."

Charles Elwood Yeager 1923-

1923 Charles Elwood Yeager is born in Myra, West Virginia. Aeroflot, largest airline in the world, is founded in the U.S.S.R. Willy Messerschmitt, German aircraft designer, establishes his aircraft factory. Edwin Huble, American astronomer, shows there are galaxies beyond the Milky Way. *Time*, a weekly news-review magazine is founded. George Gershwin writes *Rhapsody in Blue.*

1924 British Imperial Airways begins operations. China and Britain recognize the U.S.S.R. Calvin Coolidge is elected to continue as U.S. president. The U.S. bans Japanese immigrants. The first Winter Olympics are held at Chamonix, France.

1925 Adolf Hitler publishes volume I of *Mein Kampf.* Mrs. Nellie Ross, the first woman state governor, is appointed in Wyoming. The teaching of Darwin's theory of evolution is banned in Tennessee. The first solar eclipse in 300 years is seen in New York. Crossword puzzles become fashionable.

1926 Richard Byrd makes the first airplane flight to the North Pole. Amundsen, Ellsworth, and Nobile fly over North Pole to Alaska in the airship Norge. Gene Tunney wins heavyweight boxing championship from Jack Dempsey. The cork-centered baseball is introduced.

1927 Charles A. Lindbergh makes the first solo flight across Atlantic Ocean, New York to Paris in 33.5 hours. In Canada, airplanes are first used to dust crops with insecticides. Yeager's 2-year-old sister, Doris Ann, is accidently killed by brother Roy. Harlem Globetrotter's basketball team is founded by Abe Saperstein. *Show Boat,* a new kind of musical comedy, opens in New York. The first Exhibition for Space Flights opens in Moscow.

1928 Amelia Earhart is first woman to fly across Atlantic Ocean. Herbert Hoover is elected president of the U.S. Walt Disney releases his first Mickey Mouse cartoon entitled *Plane Crazy.* The first color motion pictures are exhibited by George Eastman in Rochester, New York.

1929 The U.S. stock market crash marks the end of postwar prosperity. Lieutenant James Doolittle pilots an airplane solely using instruments. Richard Byrd and three companions fly over South Pole. U.S. Army monoplane completes 150 hours in flight, refueling in air. St. Valentine's Day Massacre in Chicago sets style in gangsterism.

1930 Amy Johnson flies solo from London to Australia in 19.5 days. Crash of British airship R101 makes Britain abandon airship production. Comic strips grow in popularity in the U.S. Clyde W. Tombaugh discovers the planet Pluto.

1931 Radio waves from Milky Way are detected. The "Star Spangled Banner" officially becomes the U.S. national anthem. Swiss physicist Auguste Piccard ascends by balloon into stratosphere.

1932 Franklin D. Roosevelt is elected president in a landslide victory. Slump grows worse in U.S., 5,000 banks close, unemployment rises. Basic English proposed as an international language. "Brother Can You Spare a Dime" is a popular song. Vitamin D is discovered.

1933 British airplanes fly over Mount Everest. Roosevelt orders all banks in the U.S. closed. The 21st Amendment to the U.S. Constitution repeals Prohibition. The Chicago World's Fair opens. First baseball all-star game played. Walt Disney wins an Academy Award for his cartoon *The Three Little Pigs.*

1934 Adolf Hitler is elected Führer in Germany. Two giant ocean liners *Queen Mary* (UK) and *Normandie* (Fr) are launched. Harold Urey wins the Nobel Peace Prize for his discovery of heavy hydrogen. Max Baer wins world heavyweight boxing title.

1935 The Wagner Act, guaranteeing the worker's right to collective bargaining, becomes law. Radar equipment used to detect aircraft is developed by Robert Watson-Watts. George Gershwin's opera *Porgy and Bess* opens in New York. Roosevelt signs Social Security Act.

1936 Roosevelt is reelected by a landslide. Jesse Owens wins four gold medals at Olympic Games held in Berlin. Margaret Mitchell's *Gone With the Wind* is a runaway best-seller. Maiden flight of prototype Spitfire.

1937 Zeppelin Hindenburg is destroyed by fire in New Jersey. Amelia Earhart is lost in a Pacific flight. The first jet engine is built by Frank C. Whittle. Howard Hughes establishes a transcontinental flight record. Golden Gate Bridge, San Francisco, opens.

1938 Orson Welles panics radio public with dramatization of an invasion from Mars. HMS *Rodney* is first ship to be equipped with radar. Discovery of new nickel chrome alloy to be used in jet engines. Roosevelt appeals to Hitler and Benito Mussolini to settle European problems peaceably. 40-hour work week established in the U.S.

1939 World War II begins. Igor Sikorsky produces first serviceable helicopter. Britain operates radar stations to detect planes. Pan American Airlines begins regularly scheduled flights between the U.S. and Europe. Byrd makes his third expedition to Antarctica. Game of baseball is first televised in U.S.

1940 Germany invades Norway, Denmark, Holland, Belgium, and Luxembourg. Japan, Germany, and Italy sign military and economic pact. Roosevelt is elected president for the third time. The first helicopter flight in U.S. New combustion chamber for the jet engine designed.

1941 Japanese bomb Pearl Harbor, an American naval base in Hawaii. U.S. and Britain declare war on Japan. U.S. declares war on Germany and Italy. Yeager swears himself into the Army. First British aircraft, based on work of Whittle, flown. The "Manhattan Project" of intensive atomic research begins.

1942 The 26 Allies pledge not to make separate peace treaties with the enemies. Millions of Jews are murdered in Nazi gas chambers. Enrico Fermi splits the atom. Bell Aircraft tests the first U.S. jet. Walt Disney releases the movie *Bambi. Stars and Stripes*, a daily newspaper for U.S. forces in Europe, appears.

1943 Yeager becomes pilot; receives a pair of silver wings. U.S. troops invade Italy. President Roosevelt freezes wages, salaries, and prices to forestall inflation. Penicillin is successfully used in the treatment of chronic diseases.

1944 U.S. Allied forces invade Normandy. Yeager becomes "Ace," shooting down 13 enemy planes, 5 in one day. Yeager gets shot down over France; listed as missing in action. Later he receives Bronze Star for saving companion's life; receives Purple Heart for his wounds; earns Distinguished Flying Cross for destroying a jet fighter. The first nonstop flight takes place between London and Canada.

1945 Germany surrenders. Hitler commits suicide. The first atomic bombs are dropped on Hiroshima and Nagasaki. Japan surrenders. Roosevelt dies. Truman becomes president of U.S. Yeager marries Glennis Faye Dickhouse in Hamlin, West Virginia; they transfer to Wright Field in Dayton, Ohio.

1946 Remaining in the Army Air Force, Yeager becomes one of the first pilots to graduate from Flight Performance School. Yeager's first son, Donald, is born. Philippines are given independence by the U.S. Segregation of blacks on interstate buses declared unconstitutional.

1947 The first supersonic flight achieved by Yeager on October 14, in a U.S. Bell X-1 rocket-powered research plane named "Glamourous Glennis." More than 1 million war veterans enroll under the G.I. Bill of Rights. The *Diary of Anne Frank* is published.

1948 Yeager receives MacKay Trophy from General Hoyt S. Vandenburg, Air Force chief of staff.

President Harry S. Truman presents Yeager with the Collier Trophy for breaking sound barrier. Yeager's second son, Michael, is born.

1949 *Time* magazine of Arpil 18 features Yeager on the cover. A U.S. jet crosses the United States in 3 hours 46 minutes. NATO is formed. Muroc renamed Edwards Air Force Base in honor of Glenn Edwards. The first atomic bomb is tested in the U.S.S.R. Yeager's first daughter, Sharon, is born.

1950 Korean War begins. The U.S. recognizes Vietnam. "Glamourous Glennis" loaded under a B-29 for the last time. U.S. Atomic Energy Commission ordered by President Truman to construct hydrogen bomb. Yeager's second daughter, Susie, is born.

1951 The 22nd Amendment is passed, providing for a maximum of two terms for president and one term for vice-president succeeding to the presidency. Charles F. Blair flies solo over the North Pole. The Comet, first jet airliner, is developed in Britain.

1952 Dwight D. Eisenhower elected president of the U.S. First hydrogen bomb exploded at Eniwetok atoll, Pacific. During the month of August, 16,000 people escape from East to West Berlin.

1953 Yeager sets another speed record by flying 2.5 times the speed of sound in a Bell X-1A. Controls on wages, salaries, and some consumer goods lifted. Lung cancer reported attributable to cigarette smoking.

1954 President Eisenhower presents Yeager with Harmon International Trophy for his flight in the X-1A. Yeager leaves Edwards, is assigned to Hahn Air Base in West Germany as leader of wing gunnery team. The first controlled flight of a vertical take-off plane takes place in Britain. Racial segregation in U.S. schools is declared unconstitutional by the Supreme Court. Roger Bannister runs the first under-4-minute mile in 3 minutes 59.4 seconds.

1955 The U.S. Air Force Academy opens, modeled after West Point and Annapolis. U.S. agrees to train South Vietnamese Army. Germany becomes NATO member. U.S.S.R. creates the Warsaw Pact as rival to NATO.

1957 Yeager takes over command of a squadron of supersonic F-100 Super Sabres. Congress approves first civil-rights bill for blacks since Reconstruction. U.S.S.R. launches *Sputnik I* and *Sputnik II*, the first earth satellites. Regular London-Moscow air service begins.

1958 U.S. launches its first satellite; space race with U.S.S.R gets underway. U.S. establishes NASA, the National Aeronautics and Space Administration, to administer the scientific exploration of space. Alaska becomes 49th state. Yeager and squadron deployed to Spain.

1959 U.S.S.R. launches a rocket with two live monkeys aboard. Russian spaceship *Luna II* reaches the moon; *Luna III* photographs the "back" of the moon. World Refugee Year proclaimed. Hawaii becomes 50th state.

1960 U.S. launches its first weather satellite. Russian *Sputnik V* orbits the earth carrying two live dogs. Historic debates between presidential candidates John F. Kennedy and Richard M. Nixon; Kennedy elected. U.S. experimental rocket-powered airplane travels almost 2,000 mph.

1961 Russian cosmonaut Yuri Gagarin is first man in space. Yeager graduates top of his class from Air War College; promoted to full colonel. Alan Shepard makes the first U.S. space flight. Berlin Wall constructed.

1962 Yeager becomes commandant of the Aerospace Research Pilot School at Edwards. First American in orbit, John Glenn, makes three orbits of the earth in *Friendship 7*. Britain and France agree to construct Concorde, the first supersonic airliner.

1963   Riots, beatings, and maltreatment by officials mark civil-rights demonstrations in Birmingham, Alabama, culminating in the arrest of Martin Luther King, Jr. and in President Kennedy's calling out of troops. President Kennedy assassinated. Lyndon B. Johnson is sworn in as president.

1964   Johnson is elected president of U.S. *Ranger 7*, launched from Cape Kennedy, returns close-up photographs of the moon's surface. The Warren Commission concludes that Lee Harvey Oswald was solely responsible for the Kennedy assassination.

1965   Russian cosmonaut and American astronaut walk in space. President Johnson orders continuous bombing of North Vietnam below the 20th parallel. The official U.S. report links lung cancer with smoking. First flight around the world over both poles.

1966   Yeager is assigned as wing commander to the 405th Fighter Wing at Clark Air Force Base in the Philippines, becoming one of the few who fought in both World War II and the Vietnam War. The U.S. and U.S.S.R. agree on terms of an international treaty governing space.

1967   50,000 persons demonstrate against Vietnam War at Lincoln Memorial, Washington, D.C. Black riots in Cleveland, Newark, and Detroit. The U.S., U.S.S.R., and Britain sign a pact barring the use of nuclear weapons in space.

1968   Martin Luther King, Jr. is slain in Memphis, Tennessee. Senator Robert F. Kennedy is killed in Los Angeles, California. Richard M. Nixon is elected president. Manned U.S. spacecraft journeys 384,000 km. to the moon and back. Yeager deployed from Korea to Seymour Johnson Base in North Carolina with perfect deployment record; earns promotion to general. Yeager assigned to Germany as vice-commander of the Seventeenth Air Force.

1969   *Apollo 11* lands American astronauts on moon. Neil Armstrong first man to walk on moon. Anglo-French supersonic makes first test flight. Nationwide unrest among U.S. students causes Nixon to withdraw some troops from Vietnam.

1970   Student protests in U.S. result in killing of four by the National Guard at Kent State University in Ohio. The *Apollo 13* is checked by an explosion in midflight. Boeing 747 airliner, the jumbo jet, goes into service.

1971   Two U.S. astronauts land on moon from *Apollo 15* and drive a lunar vehicle on its surface. Yeager appointed military adviser to the Pakistani Air Force. 26th Amendment to the Constitution lowers voting age to 18.

1972   Strict anti-hijack measures are introduced internationally, especially at airports. Nixon visits Communist China. Five men are arrested trying to bug Democratic National Headquarters in Washington, D.C.; beginning of Watergate scandal. Astronomical observatories are set up on the moon by U.S. Soviet spacecraft *Venus 8* softlands on Venus.

1973   Yeager returns from Pakistan to Edwards Air Base. American *Skylab I, II,* and *III* missions completed successfully; *Skylab II* astronauts spend 28 days in space; *Skylab III* 59.5 days. Spiro T. Agnew resigns as vice-president.

1974   *Skylab IV* astronauts spend 94 days in space. U.S. Air Force SR-71 jet plane flies from New York to London in one hour, 55 minutes, 42 seconds, reaching speeds of 2,000 mph. Richard M. Nixon resigns presidency; Gerald R. Ford sworn in as president.

1975   Yeager enshrined in the Aviation Hall of Fame, the youngest member ever to be included. Yeager retires from the military with the rank of brigadier general. *Apollo* and *Soyuz* spacecraft take off for U.S.-Soviet link up in space.

1976 President Gerald R. Ford presents Yeager with Congressional Silver Medal. U.S. celebrates Bicentennial. Jimmy Carter elected president. Concorde begins trial service to Dulles, Airport, Washington, D.C.

1977 Carter pardons draft evaders. Nuclear-proliferation pact, curbing spread of nuclear weapons, signed by 15 countries including U.S.S.R. and U.S.

1978 First non-Italian Pope since 1523, Karol Cardinal Wojtyla of Poland, becomes John Paul II. The first test-tube baby born.

1979 Oil spills pollute ocean waters in Atlantic and Gulf of Mexico. Nuclear power plant accident at Three Mile Island, Pennsylvania, releases radioactivity. Soviet invasion of Afghanistan stirs world protest. Iranian militants seize U.S. Embassy in Teheran and hold hostages.

1980 Six U.S. Embassy aides escape from Iran with Canadian help. Eight servicemen killed, five injured in rescue attempt of hostages in Iran. Olympic Games in Moscow boycotted by U.S. and other nations. Ronald Reagan elected president. John Lennon of Beatles shot down in New York City.

1981 U.S.-Iran agreement frees 52 hostages held in Teheran since November 4, 1979. Ronald Reagan wounded by gunman, with press secretary and two other law enforcement officers. Pope John Paul II wounded by gunman. Sandra Day O'Conner nominated by Reagan as first woman on Supreme Court. The world's first reusable spacecraft, the shuttle *Columbia*, is sent into space.

1982 British overcome Argentina in Falklands War. Space shuttle *Columbia* lands at Edwards after successful five-day inaugural trip. Artificial heart implanted for first time in Barney B. Clark.

1983 Second space shuttle *Challenger* makes successful maiden voyage, which includes first space walk in nine years. Sally K. Ride and Air Force Colonel Guion S. Bluford, Jr., become first woman and black respectively, in space.

1984 Tom Wolfe publishes *The Right Stuff*; he feels Yeager epitomizes the spirit and attitude of what flying is all about.

1985 Bantam Books publishes Yeager's autobiography, simply titled *Yeager*.

1986 Yeager receives Horatio Alger Award, awarded to people who epitomize the spirit of the author Alger, whose books portrayed youths who rose above poverty through virtue and hard work. Space shuttle *Challenger* explodes on takeoff, killing seven on board.

INDEX- *Page numbers in boldface type indicate illustrations.*

125

ABOUT THE AUTHOR

Timothy R. Gaffney is the military and aviation writer for the *Dayton Daily News* and *The Journal Herald*, publications of Dayton Newspapers Inc. His coverage includes Wright-Patterson Air Force Base, where Chuck Yeager began his career as a test pilot. He is the author of another People of Distinction book, *Jerrold Petrofsky, Biomedical Pioneer*.

Mr. Gaffney received his bachelor of arts degree in journalism from the Ohio State University, Columbus, Ohio, in 1974. He is a student pilot and a backpacker. He lives in Miamisburg, Ohio, with his wife, Jean, their two daughters, Kimberly and Christine, and their son, Mark.

126